The Historical Series of the Reformed Church of America No. 43

Doctors for the Kingdom

The Work of the
American Mission Hospitals in the
Kingdom of Saudi Arabia

1913 - 1955

Written and Edited by
Paul L. Armerding

Foreword by Ravi K. Zacharias

WILLIAM B. EERDMANS PUBLISHING COMPANY
GRAND RAPIDS, MICHIGAN / CAMBRIDGE, U.K.

ISBN 0-8028-2683-0

Layout : Suresh Karunakaran

The Historical Series of the Reformed Church in America

The series was inaugurated in 1968 by the General Synod of the Reformed Church in
America acting through the Commission on History to communicate the church's
heritage and collective memory and to reflect on our identity and mission,
encouraging historical scholarship which informs both church and academy.

General Editor
        The Reverend Donald J. Bruggink, Ph.D.
        Western Theological Seminary

Commission on History
        James Hart Brumm, M.Div., Blooming Grove, New York
        Lynn Japinga, Ph.D., Hope College, Holland, Michigan
        Scott M. Manetsch, Ph.D., Trinity Seminary, Deerfield, Illinois
        Melody Meeter, M.Div., Brooklyn, New York
        Jesus Serrano, B.A., Norwalk, California
        Robert Terwilliger, M.Div., Kalamazoo, Michigan

Contents

Editor's Preface

The central purpose of the Historical Series of the Reformed Church in America is to serve the church. It has done so in a variety of ways. Some volumes have served the church through a scholarly analysis of portions of its past, e.g., *Sources of Secession* by Gerrit J. ten Zythoff attempted to offer an objective history of a period prior to 19th century Dutch secessionist emigration.

Other volumes have offered the history of the church in broader, but nonetheless both scholarly and accessible form, e.g., Robert Swierenga's *Dutch Chicago, A History of the Hollanders in the Windy City*, or going back to the origins of the church in America, Gerald F. DeJong's *The Dutch Reformed Church in the American Colonies*.

In the area of mission history the endeavors of the Reformed Church in America have included the magisterial volumes of Lewis R. Scudder III, *The Arabian Mission's Story, In Search of Abraham's Other Son*, and Eugene P. Heideman's *From Mission to Church, The Reformed Church in America Mission to India*, to the more popular, personal telling of mission history in *The Call of Africa*, by Morrell F. Swart.

Doctors for the Kingdom tells the story of the medical mission of the Reformed Church in America in the Kingdom of Saudi Arabia in a fast-paced, popular format, using first-person, quoted reports from the nineteenth through the twentieth century, tied together by Dr. Paul Armerding, since 1987 chief executive and surgeon of the American Mission Hospital in Bahrain. In contrast to much of the media's picture of the Muslim world, Dr. Armerding heads a hospital that holds both American and Mission in its title in a Muslim nation. The hospital receives its present support from the citizens of Bahrain, both through their use of the hospital as patients, and through the generous gifts of the people of Bahrain.

It is anticipated that this volume will receive a wide readership both in Bahrain, and in America, where both peoples may rejoice in the witness of Muslims and Christians working together for the health of the nation.

Donald J. Bruggink, General Editor,
The Historical Series of the
Reformed Church in America

Acknowledgements

Early in my career at American Mission Hospital, my curiosity about the hospital's history caused me to contact Russell Gasero, the Archivist of the Reformed Church in America. It has been a fruitful relationship as this is now the second book to spring from it. My wife Rebecca kindly assisted me with the primary research, as did Bernadette McCann. Sharon Doenitz, Faisal Al-Zamil, Hassan Al-Husseini, Maja Westra and Richard Armerding critiqued the text and offered helpful comments. Suresh Karunakaran prepared the prepublication edition of this book against tight time restraints.

Most of the photos were gathered from the archives of the Reformed Church in America and are indicated by the initials RCA. Those belonging to the hospital are indicated as AMH and those from my personal collection as PLA. My thanks to Rasul Musayeb who permitted me to use the photos of Abdulnabi Sabkar, noted as ANS.

I thank my colleagues at American Mission Hospital and the Board of Directors for allowing me to use hospital resources along with much time and energy for this project. I hope it serves to support the ongoing work and development of American Mission Hospital within Bahrain and the Arabian Gulf region.

Foreword

Ravi K. Zacharias, author of A Shattered Visage and Cries of the Heart.

The story is told of a famed sculptor first setting his eyes on the statue of Venus de Milo. He was quiet and pensive for several moments and then he said, "What is the point of such beauty—she has no hands." Charm, appeal, romance, all of these things make for attractiveness, but the hands are instruments of touch and work. This book is a story of monumental proportions because it is the story of both beauty and hands. It is a story of beauty because here life is represented in its worth and dignity. Every life, whether one is rich or poor, king or pauper is one of essential worth. The history of medical care in the Kingdom of Saudi Arabia is the story of those who cared enough to bring healing and health at a time when few dared such journeys and few were committed enough to go into these "far out places." But it is also a story of touch and work because life was hard and traveling was tough. When doctors committed to the message of Jesus Christ reached out in His name and for His sake, hospitals were built and wellness was imparted.

At times, this book reads almost like a page out of the New Testament; men, women and children coming to be touched and made well, royal families sending messages to ask for a physician to come, "upper rooms" set up in desolate places to be at the beck and call of the sick, work accomplished and the teams move on to other parts. As you read this history of a mission hospital and of medical practitioners you will be transported into a different time and your heart will be lifted to think in soul-searching depth. Words cannot fully convey a story but they are the best tools we have. Here we have not only words, but a handful of pictures and, yes, even stones that if only they could speak would tell lofty tales of faith and courage. I wish there were more books like this to lift us beyond our small worlds to places of need. I am convinced that many of the conflicts in our world today would at least be mitigated if our hands reached out in a similar fashion to the story told here.

There is an island in Hawaii, called Molokai. There, for many years the Belgian missionary, Joseph Damien, labored to work with people who had leprosy. In the end, he contracted it himself. If you go today to that island you will see a grave with his name on it. But upon questioning you find out that he is really not buried there, but in Belgium where his family and the government wanted back their hero. Those in Molokai pleaded that he be buried among the people he had served. When they were denied they asked that at least his right arm be severed and buried in Molokai. Their request was granted. In the end, the hand that had touched them was buried in the grave they had lovingly prepared.

I thought of that story when I read *Doctors For The Kingdom*. They loved and touched many lives. Their legacy continues today in other parts of the world. As you read, your heart will be stirred and may your hands reach out to a needy world. Dr. Armerding's effort to keep this story in our memory is a noble piece of work and worthy of our study. It is a story of beauty that will touch your life.

Paul L. Armerding

Preface

We live in an era that affords easy travel and we have a
variety of sophisticated tools for communication. In spite
of these, many Americans remain ignorant and even fearful of
Arabs, and vice-versa. What often seems to be lacking in the
equation is a simple appreciation that people everywhere are little
different from one another. That is not to minimize the differences
created by religion, worldview, experience or exposure. However,
these are often blown out of proportion, and the basic areas where we
share common experiences, values and goals are overlooked.

This little book is an attempt to create some understanding. In the
pages that follow is the story of several Americans and one
Englishman who chose to live and work in Arabia in the early
years of the twentieth century. Having experienced the grace
of God in their own lives, they wished to share it in practical
ways with their neighbors in the Arabian Peninsula.
Likewise, it was a small group of leaders among the
Gulf Arabs who appreciated what was being
offered and took advantage of it for the
sake of their people.

In telling this story, I have chosen to interject
some pieces of creative writing to make the
account more interesting and to fill in some gaps. There
is an element of supposition in these parts, but nowhere
do such additions add materially to the story. The stories
and incidents are all true. In fact, large parts of several stories
have been left in the words of the key actors. They were highly
literate people and faithfully recorded their experiences. I cannot
improve on what they said. Therefore, I list myself as the author /
editor of this volume.

My hope is that both Americans and Gulf Arabs will read and enjoy
this book, and appreciate each other more for the experience. We
have much to learn from each other. A touch of humility and a
willingness to take each other at face value will do all of us
good, just as it did for the people in this story.

"When you enter a town,

eat what is set before you.

Heal the sick and tell them,

'The kingdom of God is near you.'"

Jesus the Prophet (Peace be upon Him)

as quoted by

Luke the Physician

Introduction

As the 19th century came to a close, exciting new developments were taking place in the field of medicine. Earlier, the Renaissance and the Reformation movements in Europe had led to a revival of interest in classical writings on medicine such as those of Hippocrates and Ibn Sina

(Avicenna). New discoveries were quickly adding to or correcting the works of the past. But this progress in scientific knowledge was primarily benefiting Europe and North America.

The founders of the Arabian Mission -
{L-R} James Cantine, Prof. Lansing and
Samuel Zwemer [RCA]

There were, however, small groups of people in the churches of North America and Europe who were concerned for both the spiritual and physical welfare of their fellow humans. One such group originated in the year 1889 in the city of New Brunswick, New Jersey, USA, and adopted the name "Arabian Mission." In Arabia, they came to be known as the "American Mission."

The pioneers of the American Mission first established themselves in Basrah, Iraq, in the year 1891. As they worked in Basrah and visited other parts of the Arabian Gulf, the need for modern medical services became apparent. They called for doctors and nurses to join them and began providing itinerant services among their stations.

With permission from HH *Shaikh* Isa bin Ali Al-Khalifa, property was obtained in Bahrain and the first hospital of the American Mission was erected in 1902. The family of DeWitt Mason of New York contributed the funds for this project so the hospital was named Mason Memorial Hospital. It was formally dedicated "to God and Arabia" on January 26, 1903. In time, more hospitals were built in Iraq, Kuwait and Oman.

Dr. Sharon J. Thoms [RCA]

Dr. Marion Wells Thoms [RCA]

Dr. Sharon Thoms and Dr. Marion Wells Thoms were the first doctors to staff the newly built Mason Memorial Hospital in Bahrain.

Sadly, Dr. Marion Wells Thoms died of typhoid fever during the summer of 1905. When later a second hospital was erected in Bahrain for the care of women and children, it was named the Marion Wells Thoms Memorial Hospital in her honor. Dr. Sharon Thoms then transferred to Oman. In Bahrain, he was followed by Drs. Stanley Mylrea, Paul Harrison, Louis Dame, Harold Storm, Wells Thoms, Esther Barny Ames, Gerald Nykerk and Bernard Voss to name just a few.

Marion Wells Thoms Memorial Hospital circa-1927 [RCA]

In the early years of the twentieth century, the Ottoman Turks prevented personnel of the American Mission from conducting activities outside of their coastal stations. However, when *Shaikh* Abdulaziz Al Saud began to exert his influence over the greater part of the Arabian Peninsula, the situation changed. The remaining Turks were evicted from Eastern Arabia by April of 1913, and *Shaikh* Abdulaziz installed new leaders to bring order in this region. The Governor of Al-Hasa, Ibn Jalawi, and the ruling *sheyukh* of other cities in Eastern Saudi Arabia began inviting the mission doctors from Bahrain to provide services for them and their people. Although initially suspicious of the missionaries' intentions, in time relationships of trust developed and a fairly regular pattern of medical visits was established.

In the course of their visits, the mission doctors witnessed the start of the petroleum industry in the Kingdom of Saudi Arabia and the opportunities this created for the country. One of the benefits was the establishment of oil company, and later, government-sponsored medical services that eventually supplanted the work being done by the mission hospitals from

Bahrain. The mission hospitals' work in the Kingdom was discontinued after 1955.

An engraving showing the New Brunswick Seminary of the Reformed Church in America [RCA]

In the forty-two year period during which the Mason Memorial and the Thoms Memorial Hospitals in Bahrain served the Kingdom of Saudi Arabia and its rulers, over 275,000 patients were treated in temporary clinics while another 17,500 were treated in their homes. Approximately 3,500 major and 14,000 minor surgical operations were performed. Taken altogether, the mission doctors and hospital staff provided at least 96 months or the equivalent of 8 full years of medical services within the Kingdom.

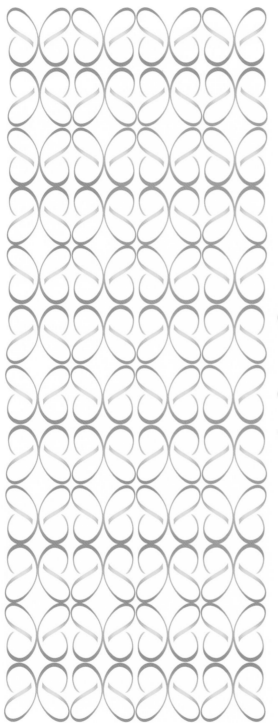

Chapter 1

*Before the
King Came
Before the
Mission Visited*

He wondered if some experience in America's "Wild West" would have been better preparation for Arabia.

As he walked through the arched doorway of Mason Memorial Hospital that Sunday morning, the sight that greeted his eyes was as bad as he had imagined. In Dr. Mylrea's own words, this was the scene:

The Operating Room at the Mason Memorial Hospital circa 1904 [RCA]

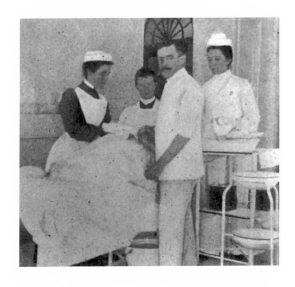

"When I reached the hospital, the wounded men and their friends seemed to fill the whole house. It appeared that there had been one of the periodic raids which are the curse of Arabia. The Bedouins around Katif, a province on the mainland, having found out that certain Katifis had got together a considerable sum of money for the [pearl] diving season, promptly came down upon them and attacked them; killed thirty-two and wounded ten more, and apparently got away with their loot. The Bedouins also lost heavily, I believe, but no one seems to have any particulars, since they carried away all the dead and wounded with them. The big sheikh of the place immediately gave orders that all the wounded men were to be put onto a boat and sent over to us [in Bahrain].

"In a very short time Mrs. Zwemer was at work getting them ready for the operating room. Their ideas of first aid to the wounded are meagre, to say the least, and from appearances one felt that they had picked out the very dirtiest rags they could find for dressing compound fractures and gaping gunshot injuries. One wound at least was swarming with maggots, although the fight had occurred only three days before. After a while every one was at work --

Dr. Iverson at the chloroform bottle and Mrs. Zwemer as chief assistant -- unfortunately my chief native helper was ill. For five hours straight we worked and finally sat down to breakfast at the rather late hour of 2:30 PM.

Dr. C. Stanley G. Mylrea in the ward of the Mason Memorial Hospital, circa - 1907 [RCA]

One man had his left collarbone shattered in the center, the ball finally lodging in the muscles of the shoulder, from whence it was removed by incision. As his antagonist had discharged his rifle at a distance of about six feet, all the neighborhood of the wound was charred. In addition, he had received a nasty stab wound in the chest. Another man had his right hand badly smashed. We removed a lot of bone, and he will, we hope, quite recover, but I am afraid he will never again have a strong right hand. Another man was shot through both hips; from him we also removed a bullet, as well as a felt wad, but as he was an elderly man and had sustained tremendous shock, he died on the fifth day. Another was shot through the back, and received internal injuries, and now lies in a critical condition. Another had his leg smashed, and we were obliged to take out some half-dozen large pieces of bone. Still another had his left elbow joint shattered, and there was nothing to do but to reset practically the entire joint. This was one of the wounds that had maggots in it. This patient was also hit in the back, and so on and so on. Out of the ten we hope to save eight." ["Hospital Experiences", *Neglected Arabia*, Number 78, July-September 1911, pp. 11-14]

Samuel M. Zwemer - the first member of the mission to visit mainland Arabia [RCA]

In the eight years since Mason Memorial Hospital had opened, its reputation had spread beyond the shores of Bahrain Island to the Arabian mainland. A steady trickle of patients came mainly from the eastern shore of the peninsula although from time to time people from the Nejd region further inland also arrived seeking treatment. By far the majority of these patients were men. For most Arabs living on the mainland, the services of Mason Memorial Hospital were out of reach. Samuel Zwemer, one of the founders of the American Mission, had managed to make some brief visits to Eastern Arabia in the 1890's. More recently, however, he had been turned back on three attempts to enter the mainland at the customs port of Uqair. The Turkish rulers of the Arabian Peninsula showed little interest in maintaining law and order and they were not inclined to allow outsiders to bring needed services into the territories they controlled.

In 1913, the ruling order changed in eastern Arabia. *Shaikh* Abdulaziz Al Saud carried his conquests to the eastern shore and installed his cousin, Abdulla Ibn Jalawi as governor. The new governor, ruling from Hofuf, wasted no time in imposing law and order. His rule was impartial and fair; one law applied to all persons. Punishments were harsh and administered promptly. In very little time, banditry ceased, and the Eastern Province of the young Kingdom of Saudi Arabia became one of the safest places on earth.

For the medical staff of Mason Memorial Hospital in Bahrain, this change in government heralded a new day. In 1913, the first invitation came for a doctor to visit Qatif. Dr. Paul Harrison responded and spent a busy month treating members of the local *shaikh's* household as well as the general public. A new chapter had opened in the history of the American Mission.

At the gate of the Mason Memorial Hospital, Bahrain [RCA]

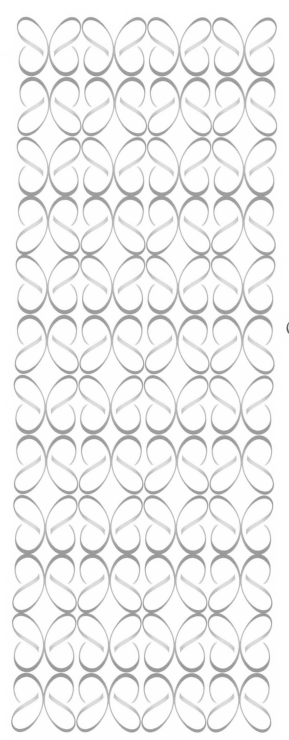

Chapter 2

Early Days

Dr. Paul W. Harrison
as a young surgeon [RCA]

It was June 22, 1914. Dr. Paul Harrison knew this because he had brought a calendar with him from Bahrain. There were no newspapers in Qatif. He adjusted the Primus lantern and hung it from a nail above his writing table. His office this evening was on the veranda facing the sea. Fortunately, there was a breeze from the north offering relief from the early summer heat. Paul sat down, wiped the sweat from his brow, and relaxed for several minutes just enjoying the feel of the wind as it dried the moisture on his body.

Paul thought back over the past 6 years since he had graduated from Johns Hopkins University-College of Medicine in the United States. After spending two years as a house officer at Massachusetts General Hospital in Boston, he had traveled to Basrah, Iraq, to learn Arabic and had done well in the two-year course. Daily he was putting his medical and linguistic skills to work as he cared for patients in Bahrain. Now he was visiting the territory recently annexed by *Shaikh* Abdulaziz Al Saud, *Sultan* of the Nejd and its Dependencies.

Today, Paul had seen several residents of Qatif. Some had tuberculosis and probably would not live much longer. He had offered them the best advice he could, hoping that rest, gentle exercise and better nutrition might help. Above all, he had advised them to stop smoking and to stay away from the smoke of their cooking fires.

*A young Arab patient
[RCA]*

Others had eyes inflamed with trachoma. He had started them on a regular regimen of eye drops. Paul wondered how many would keep it up for the full course of treatment. There had been children with diarrhea -- common at this time of year. He had gently counseled their veiled mothers to give these little ones plenty of oral fluids. Tomorrow, he would perform surgery on a man with a large hernia. Paul mapped out a strategy to keep the ubiquitous flies away from his patient's wound.

A year ago, the people of Qatif had been pleased to host the doctor on his first visit. They were aware of the Mason Memorial Hospital, which had been established in Manama, Bahrain, eleven years ago. A number had visited the hospital and received treatment there. Now a doctor was coming to them. His visit of six weeks was so much better than no doctor at all.

Several minutes had passed and Paul felt cooler and more comfortable. He uncapped his pen and began to write a letter. In the middle of it he briefly described his present circumstances in Qatif:

"The work here has been very satisfactory. About 1/2 the volume of an equally long stay last summer, which is really very good. I am hoping to get further inland before I come out." [Letter to Dr. Chamberlain of the RCA Board of Missions]

Dr. Harrison later wrote a summary account of the Bahrain medical work in 1914 and included these comments:

"...Bin Saoud sent several of his men for treatment."

"We spent a month and a half in Kateef.... Medical clinics were large, indeed, at first quite overwhelming. A good amount of operating was done, including some major work." ["Bahrain Medical Work, 1914", *The Christian Intelligencer*, January 20, 1915; pp. 41-42]

Chapter 3

*A Doctor
Meets the
King*

Dr. C. Stanley G. Mylrea
[RCA]

Dr. Stanley Mylrea had not planned a busy day. It was Sunday, a day he normally devoted to worship and rest. But this Sunday, early in May, 1914, would be different. *Shaikh* Mubarrak had sent a message to Dr. Mylrea's house the evening before. The *Shaikh's* car was not functioning; therefore, a horse coach would arrive soon and take the doctor to the camp of *Shaikh* Abdulaziz Al Saud who was camped thirty-three kilometers outside Kuwait City.

The coach arrived quite early and Dr. Mylrea set out with his medical bag in hand. He carried a large supply of quinine tablets, for he had been informed that many of *Shaikh* Abdulaziz's men were sick with the fever -- most likely malaria contracted in Al-Hasa. The ride was interrupted only once midway to change horses. Dr. Mylrea later recounted his experiences that day with these words:

"It was a glorious cool day with bright sunshine and I shall always remember the thrill with which I drove into Ibn Saud's camp. It consisted principally of a street of white European tents of the E. P. type. At the far end of the street, across it and closing it, was the tent of my host. It was a very large marquee in the door of which stood Ibn Saud, waiting to greet me.

King Abdulaziz Abdulrahman Al-Saud with retainers early in his reign [RCA]

"I alighted from the carriage and we entered his tent together. There was no one in it. It was superbly furnished in the desert Arab style. The floor was completely covered with carpets, and at intervals against the tent wall and at right angles to it were camel saddles covered by beautiful white sheep skins. These are very comfortable to lean against when sitting on the floor. Hanging up against the walls were plenty of good rifles, shiny and bright. Everything was business-like, orderly,

and handsome. Somehow the tent breathed security, confidence and efficiency, just as did its master as he and I greeted each other.

"He was indeed a notable personality, of commanding height - well over six feet - and beautifully yet simply dressed in a long white robe over which he wore a brown cloak heavily embroidered with gold thread. On his head was the regulation kerchief and double rope. His feet were bare, for he had left his sandals at the threshold as we came in. He appeared to be in perfect health and I guessed his age to be about thirty-five. He impressed me immensely. Every line of him, face and figure told of intelligence, energy, determination, and reserves of compelling power. It was a good face too which bore witness to his reputation as a man of deep piety and devotion. It was not the face of a profligate upstart, but the face of a man who had disciplined himself and knew what it was to fast and to pray. Finally, he was obviously an aristocrat in whose veins flowed the bluest blood in Arabia. It is probable that all Europeans and Americans who have come under the sway of the remarkable Arab would sum him up in much the same words. His career during the past thirty-five years has borne ever increasing testimony to the correctness of those impressions made upon me so long ago."

"Ibn Saud and I did not linger. A cup of coffee and I excused myself to go and see the sick men." [*Kuwait Before Oil* -- the memoirs of Dr. C. Stanley G. Mylrea (unpublished), 1951, pp. 66-68]

Chapter 4

First Invitations to Riyadh

Dr. Paul W. Harrison
in traditional Arab dress
all set for crossing the desert [RCA]

The afternoon sun was descending rapidly. As shadows lengthened outside on that July evening in 1917, the available light inside the operating room diminished. More lights could be added except that they would raise the temperature in the room still further. Dr. Paul Harrison was glad that the patient on the table was his last case of the day. Surgery was a demanding task at any time, but especially on a July afternoon. Just a few more sutures and this case would be finished. Paul was already planning his evening.

An assistant opened the door of the operating room. "Dr. Harrison" he said, "this special envelope was just delivered for you." Paul left it for his surgical assistant to bandage the wound. He stepped outside, removed his rubber gloves, and wiped his face and hands with a towel. He opened the large, embossed envelope with anticipation and was not disappointed. Here, at last, was an official invitation from *Shaikh* Abdulaziz Al Saud to visit the capital city of the Nejd--Riyadh.

On board a sailing ship from Bahrain to Uqair [RCA]

After a brief stop at his house, Paul went looking for the British Consul whose official permission was required for such a trip. In less than forty-eight hours, permission was granted and baggage was packed. With one assistant from the hospital to accompany him, Paul set out from Bahrain by boat to Uqair on the Saudi coast. There followed a trip that would be repeated many more times by the hospital teams -- one day from Uqair to Hofuf, several days rest in the oasis of Hofuf, then several more days overland to Riyadh. In the early years, donkeys were used for the first stage of this trip and camels for the second. Later, trucks and automobiles became available making the trip both faster and more comfortable.

Mrs. Harrison later recorded Paul's memories of his first meeting with *Shaikh* Abdulaziz Al Saud.

A camel caravan en route to Riyadh [RCA]

"Ibn Saud was standing in a small unpretentious room. He met Paul with a cordial handshake and the simple greeting, 'Peace be upon you.' Paul replied, 'And on you be peace.'

"'While you are here, my house is yours,' added the sheikh, motioning for Paul to sit down with him. A slave brought in coffee, and while Ibn Saud sipped his, he explained that he had asked the doctor to come in, not for his health nor the health of his family, but for the needs of his people. He had arranged a nearby house for a hospital. He wanted his people treated without cost to them. 'You may find some of my Bedouin hostile, but that needn't trouble you. You are a guest in my house, and no harm can come to you. I know you are a Christian, but honorable men are friends though they differ in religion. I met your fellow doctor in Kuwait years ago when he treated some of my men. Captain Shakespeare and Captain Cox have been in here, and I respect them.'

"'I bring you the greetings of all my colleagues.'

"'There is one other thing,' said Ibn Saud, smiling. 'If you want to smoke in my house, you may do so.'

"Paul laughed. 'I do not use tobacco, but I have an assistant who will be most glad for your kind offer.'

"'I see you think of those under you. It is the same with me. Even a ruler is the servant of his people.'" [Ann Monteith Harrison, *A Tool in His Hand*, pp. 78-79]

In a letter sent to his supporters in the USA, Paul Harrison summarized this first inland trip.

A patient from the Nejd visiting the Mason Memorial Hospital
[RCA]

"We stayed in Riadh for twenty days, and had more medical work than could possibly be attended to. A considerable amount of operating was done. Two difficult stone cases were lost, but this did not appear to affect the reputation of the work a great deal, and when we stopped because our stock of medicine was exhausted, there was a great demand for all sorts of surgical work, a demand which could only be met by inviting the patients to come to Bahrein." ["The Tour to Riadh", *Neglected Arabia*, Number 104, January-March 1918, p. 5]

*The Capital of the Nejd, Riyadh
as it appeared in the 1920's
[RCA]*

*Donkeys taking a break
[RCA]*

Dr. Harrison's second invitation to Riyadh arrived with greater urgency attached to it. In the winter of 1919, a world-wide epidemic of influenza took many lives. Even the vast expanses of the Arabian Desert did not prevent it from reaching Riyadh. By the time Paul arrived at the capital city, the *Sultan* had already lost his eldest son, Turki, and his wife, Jawhara bint Musaid, to influenza. In spite of this, Paul was able to bring comfort and assistance to many other sufferers, most of whom survived. During this visit, he also helped organize better distribution of food and supplies in Riyadh.

*Dr. Louis Paul Dame
as a young surgeon [RCA]*

When a third invitation arrived in the final months of 1920, Dr. Harrison was unavailable. The opportunity was taken by a new doctor at Mason Memorial Hospital, Louis Paul Dame. In time, Dr. Dame became a frequent visitor to Riyadh and inland Arabia. He became quite famous for his accomplishments. His first visit was a routine but busy affair of which he left a detailed record. His first and deepest impressions of this trip were of the resistance he encountered. But with the support of *Shaikh* Abdulaziz, Dr. Dame and his assistants ran clinics in a house for several days and in time won many friends. Like his colleagues who had met *Shaikh* Abdulaziz Al Saud before him, Louis Dame was impressed by his host.

"Sheikh Abdul Aziz is by far the finest Arab I have met. He is at least six feet two, powerfully built, possessing a most intelligent face and a very charming smile. He is most kingly in his bearing. There is never any mistaking the man. And he is not an idler. He sits in a mejlis (reception room, of which he has many), and receives his subjects, rich or poor, Bedouin or townsman; all can come and present their troubles or their gifts. Then he sits in his office, where he keeps four secretaries busy, and reads the official mail and dictates his affairs. The Arab is not naturally a democrat, but there is a democratic spirit to this government. It has much of the old patriarchal type." ["Intolerance in Inland Arabia", *Neglected Arabia*, Number 117, April-June 1921, p. 11]

Four Elders of the Ikhwan in Riyadh
[RCA]

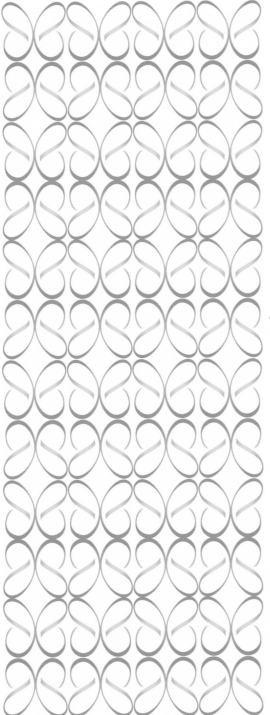

Chapter 5

A Doctor
Saves the
King

*Dr. Louis Dame
on his way to
Riyadh
[RCA]*

r. Louis Dame was glad for a quiet day. It was Tuesday morning, December 24, 1923. The medical team had ended its work in Riyadh, and his assistants were preparing to depart. He needed a restful day before travel and welcomed the opportunity to bring his diary up to date. The sun was shining through the east-facing window of his room. He had been a guest in the palace of *Shaikh* Abdulaziz Al Saud for the past five weeks. As the *Sultan* had promised, the medical party would proceed further inland tomorrow.

"What a year this has been", Louis thought to himself. In the spring, the *Sultan* had called him from Bahrain to Al-Hasa to treat a persistent sore throat. He had swabbed gentian violet on *Shaikh*

Abdulaziz's inflamed tissues under the watchful eye of Ibn Jalawi, the Governor of Eastern Province. The *Sultan* had recovered and was grateful for the doctor's attendance. Unfortunately, Dr. Dame had contracted typhoid fever and had fallen ill shortly after returning to Bahrain. It had taken a month of rest in the cool heights of Kodaikanal, South India, away from the summer heat of the Gulf, for him to recover. He had regained most of his strength by the time the *Sultan* called him to Riyadh at the beginning of November.

Louis pulled the curtains back and let the sun pour into his room. The warmth felt good and the light aided his writing. What had begun five weeks ago as a routine trip had quickly become an exciting challenge. By all measures, it had been a more satisfying experience than his previous visit to Riyadh. Dr. Dame wrote:

"We were invited to Nejd by the Sultan particularly to treat the Sultan's aged father. We left Bahrein on November 6th with four hospital helpers and thirty-two boxes of medicines and supplies. We left Hassa early Monday morning, November 12th, and on the next day in the afternoon were met by two special messengers of the Sultan on fast trotting camels with a letter for me. It requested me to proceed with all possible haste to the Sultan who was seriously ill with some swelling of the face. Fortunately I was riding a 'dhalool' (trotting camel, or dromedary) and after opening up a few boxes and taking a few needed supplies, one of the riders and one of my assistants with me started out after an early supper. That night we traveled till nearly midnight and were up again before dawn. We stopped for about an hour in the middle of the forenoon for a combined

breakfast and lunch. We then rode again till about an hour before sunset and rested for an hour for supper. Then we rode again till nearly midnight, etc. Both Wednesday and Thursday we were actually in the saddle over fifteen hours. Friday afternoon at about three p.m. we arrived in Riadh and I was at once ushered before the Sultan. I found him to be suffering from a cellulitis of the face. His face was tremendously swollen, his eye was the size of a baseball and his lips were so swollen that he could hardly speak. I barely recognized him. He was so different from the usual energetic, enthusiastic Abd el Aziz ibn Saud. It was really pathetic to see him and he muttered as best he could, 'Oh my friend, I was afraid you wouldn't come in time. I surrender myself in your hands; whatever you want to do, do.'

Central Riyadh in the 1920's [RCA]

"You may be sure that I at once got busy. I was in attendance for an hour every forenoon, afternoon and evening. It was necessary to lance the swelling in three places. The *following Thursday he was well enough to hold a public reception to which the whole town and hundreds of Bedouins turned out. I should roughly guess that about 5,000 people streamed into the reception hall during the forenoon. It was very interesting to watch from a well hidden observatory. The next day he attended the big Friday prayers at the large mosque. He had not been able to attend for four Fridays previously because of this infection. He continued to improve and within another few days was much improved and is today quite himself again."* ["Touring Inland Arabia", *Neglected Arabia*, Number 130, July-September 1924, pp. 3-4]

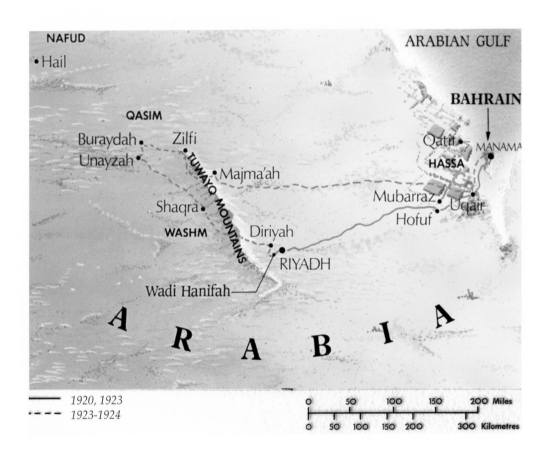

*The route of Dr. Louis Dame's travels through Central Arabia
in 1920 and 1923 - 1924
[AMH]*

Chapter 6

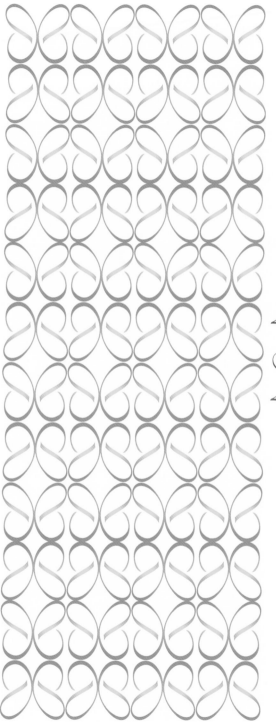

Adventures Further Afield

ℱr. Louis Dame felt satisfied with the work he and his colleagues had accomplished over the past few weeks. "Today might be Christmas Eve," Louis thought to himself, "but you would never know that in Riyadh." He missed his wife Betty and his friends who were back in Bahrain. He was glad that tomorrow, Christmas day, would be busy. Their equipment along with the remaining medicines and supplies were being placed back into travelling cases ready for loading onto camels in the morning.

King Abdul Aziz in his Crossley automobile in 1924.
[RCA]

Apart from treating the *Sultan*, Dr. Dame had this to say about his 1923 visit to Riyadh:

"We were then able to get to work in our dispensary. We were given a good house

A large camel caravan in central Arabia
[RCA]

and living quarters for the hospital helpers. I continued to live at the castle. In twenty-seven actual working days we made 3,374 treatments of which 1,306 were new cases and 1,978 were re-treatments and 90 outcalls. We performed 36 major operations and 101 minor operations and gave 15 intravenous injections.

"We were very well received and have been very well treated.... The attitude of patients coming for treatment was so much more cordial and they showed more confidence in us. Almost all operative cases were perfectly willing to be operated on when I suggested operating. The usual answer was, 'As you like; when do you want to operate, now?' Usually a delay of a day or even a half a day was demurred at. 'Why not now?' This seemed to be Hassa and not Riyadh." ["Touring Inland Arabia", *Neglected Arabia*, Number 130, July-September 1924, pp. 4-5]

The Ruins of the old Al-Saud capital city of Diriyah in Wadi Al-Hanifa as they appear today.
[PLA]

A well in the midst of date palms in Wadi Al-Hanifa
[PLA]

The following morning broke cool and clear. There was a light wind from the north. The camel caravan wound its way out of Riyadh and up the *Wadi* Al-Hanifa. Louis Dame swayed back and forth gently in his saddle. Like speaking Arabic, riding a camel was part of his life now. As he passed the sun-bleached ruins of Diriyah, he wondered if the famous *magi* had passed this same way 1900 years before. Like them, he came bearing gifts. His gifts were not the gold, frankincense and myrrh that were traditionally carried on these routes. He came with medicine, knowledge and the skilled hands of a surgeon. Hopefully, these gifts would be as well received in Shaqra, Oneiza and Buraidah as they had been in Al-Hasa and Riyadh.

The minaret of the mosque in Oneiza in the 1920s.
[RCA]

Indeed, both the hospital personnel and their gifts were well received. There was some hesitation initially, and several citizens were not sure they wanted to associate with the outsiders. But overall it was a positive experience, about

which Dr. Dame said,

"We remained in Shugra sixteen days. During twelve working days we treated 953 patients, did 32 major and 16 minor operations, and gave 19 Neo-salvarsan injections....The religious Sheikh and his son were both operated on for hernia, and of all the people I met on this tour old Sheikh Ibrahim stands highest in my estimation. He is a most devout Moslem, but a sincere one. He was honestly worried about my soul and tried his best to convert me. He urged me to read the Koran-'the Word of God,' 'the light of life' which would be a blessing to me in this world and in the life to come. He was a real friend to the day we left, though neither persuaded the other to change his religion."

Dr. Dame performing surgery in Hofuf in 1924 [RCA]

"Nowhere were we treated as royally as at Aneiza. Frequently we were the guests of some of the leading families for meals, and every evening we made two or three social visits and were obliged to turn down as many more. Our evenings were usually booked a week ahead.... Everywhere we were greeted and treated cordially

and here as in every place the streets leading to our house were always lined with the blind, crippled, and the sick who were seeking relief. We remained in Aneiza twenty-two days, and in seventeen working days treated 1,366 clinic patients, did 53 major operations, 89 minor operations, and gave 34 Neo-salvarsan injections. We saw a great many patients in their homes, as frequently our social calls were mixed with professional calls, but no record was kept of the patients thus seen. Upon leaving we were loaded with tins of dates and a particularly fine cooky [keyijja] for desert travelling."

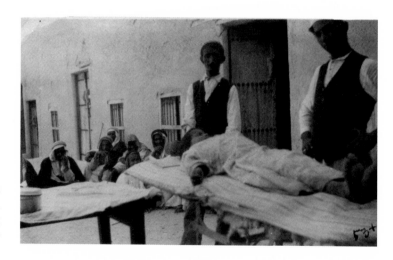

Helpers and observers in the operating room, Hofuf, 1924 [RCA]

"On Monday, February 11th [1924], we left Aneiza for Boreida, where we arrived that afternoon, for this is only a six-hour journey...."

"We had decided to remain in Boreida only about a week as it was time to return to Bahrein. Our supply of medicine was running low...and plague had broken out in Bahrein. In the last two months we had received mail from Bahrein only twice, the last one telling us about plague. So you can understand that we were

anxious to return. We had received invitations to visit Rass, Hail and Mejma, and although we would have had to have permission from the Sultan for these visits, that would without doubt have been granted. But we had to turn down all invitations."

Women waiting to be
seen by a doctor in
Hofuf, in 1924.
[RCA]

"We remained in Boreida only ten days and in seven working days treated 859 clinic patients, performed 7 major and 8 minor operations and gave 13 Neo-salvarsan injections.

"On Thursday, February 21st, we started out on our long return journey. We were bound for Hassa, for the routes to Kuweit and Jebeel were unsafe because of some Bedouin uprising. We had with us four soldiers of the Sultan, two of whom had come with us from Riadh and two more were given us at Boreida. We passed through Zulfie, then passed over the Tuweik mountain range, passed some Ikhwan settlements and the town of Mejma. From here we kept in a straight southeast

A crowd of patients waiting outside the clinic in Hofuf, 1924 [RCA]

An overhead view of the surgical area, Hofuf, 1924 [RCA]

The post surgical recovery area in Hofuf, 1924 [RCA]

direction till we arrived at Hassa on the eighteenth day after leaving Boreida. The Camel Express is a long weary journey, but fortunately there is an end to all things. We did not stop in Hassa but at once pushed on for Ojeir and Bahrein. While at sea we lay at anchor two days because of a strong contrary wind but finally succeeded in making the wrong end of Bahrein Island. We walked five hours and arrived at the country castle of Sheikh Hamed who was kind enough to send us home in his Ford.

"An interesting numerical report of our trip might be mentioned. In Riadh we are now fairly well known but we were the first doctors ever to have come to any of the other places. Yet the total number of clinic patients treated during the tour was 6,552, total major operations 128, total minor operations 214, and Neo-salvarsans 81. Forty-one days of the four months and seven days were spent in travelling, practically all on the camel." ["Entering New Territory", *Neglected Arabia*, Number 131, October-December 1924, pp.4-7]

Two Arab patients
[RCA]

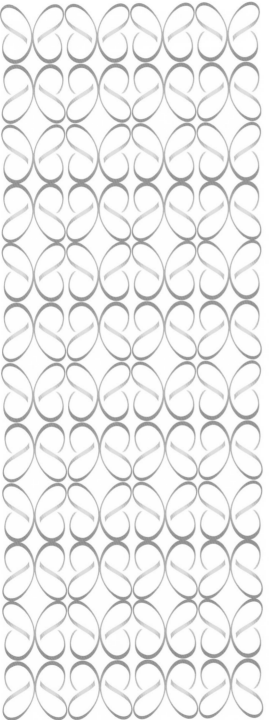

Chapter 7

*Westward
to the
Hejaz*

$\mathcal{C}$onditions changed rapidly over the next few years. These changes are evident in Dr. Dame's account of his experiences touring across the peninsula in 1932:

"On Thursday evening, May 19th, a messenger came from the Gosabies, (Bahrain agents for Ibn Saoud) saying that a telegram had just come from the King asking me to come at once to Taif, Hedjaz, to treat a member of his family. On Friday, all preparations were made, our baggage put in a launch which then sailed round the island to Zillag and at midnight we went aboard there. The next morning just after sunrise we arrived at Ojeir. A car was waiting for us and after arranging for our baggage which had to go by donkeys, we were off. In two hours and twenty minutes we were in Hofhuf. We spent the day there calling on friends and waiting for baggage. Lorries were sent to the edge of the sand-dunes to meet our baggage and returned with it in the afternoon. On the morning of the 22nd, we started the trip, almost across the peninsula in extent. We left Hofhuf about 8:30 with a Chevrolet touring-car and two lorries, one a Chevy and the other a Ford. We carried petrol, water and food sufficient to get us to Riadh if necessary, though we did replenish our water at two wells and bought a sheep for dinner at one of the wells.

"We arrived at the small town of 'Arier shortly after noon and rested for about an hour. Three other cars were there, large open buses, en route to Hassa from the Hedjaz. There were twenty passengers, fourteen of whom were young Hedjazies who had learned to operate wireless telegraphy and who were going to man the wireless stations or relieve men already at work at Hassa, Ojeir, Katif and Jubail."

Busses used for cross-desert travel in Saudi Arabia in the 1930's
[RCA]

"From 'Arier on we had a very bad stretch of desert-sand, hummocks and ruts, and we made very slow progress. Our lorries got stuck several times and all hands (20 pairs in all) were required to push them out. One of them had engine trouble, too. We lost this one eventually and spent some time looking for it. It would have taken several hours to repair its damages, so we took off most of its load and went on without it.

"We spent the first night in Wadi Jidda and the second night at Wadi Et Tairie. Here were a couple of wells and also some rain water in a deep ravine. We cooked our supper, made coffee and then drove a safe distance from the Wadi to sleep, for there were many mosquitoes and sand flies. There was considerable vegetation here, mostly acacia trees.

"We had not followed the usual caravan route between Hassa and Riadh so did not strike Abu Jifan. We were about forty or fifty miles north of that route and thus avoided the sand dunes of the Dahna. The Dahna here was sandy but quite level and not very hard to cross. The next morning at eight o'clock we arrived in Riadh just forty-eight hours after we had left Hofhuf. We had traveled just about half of that time, taking twenty-four hours to do three hundred miles, or just less than fifteen miles per hour. This part was by far the worst stretch of the road; beyond Riadh we made better time. I was surprised at the definite roadway, not a macadam roadway, but made only by tracks of numerous cars. A telegram had been sent from Hofhuf, at our departure, so Riadh knew when to expect us. The

A view of the Dahna sands as they appear today
[PLA]

same telegram had been sent to the King in Taif and he had directed the Crown Prince, Amir Saoud, to have me examine his (the King's) five small sons and then to speed me on, not to allow me more than two hours in Riadh.

Crown Prince Saud ibn Abdulaziz
Al-Saud with two of his brothers
[RCA]

"The Amir Saoud resembles his father more than ever. He has the same cordial greeting for visitors that the King has and that same charming smile. I was given the same room in the Palace that I occupied in 1923, and at once swarms of visitors and patients came in. We were soon invited to lunch with the Amir and five members of the Rashid family who as permanent prisoner guests dine with the Amir daily. Then I saw the five young princes, several more patients, and was taken by the Amir to his summer palace on the Wadi Hanifa, near Deraiyah, where his ancestors ruled years ago. The Amir and a younger brother wanted examinations. We were shown around the Amir's very fine gardens as well as the palace and then departed.

"Another car joined our party, also bound for Taif. We left Riadh at 1 p.m. We had been held up five hours instead of two as ordered by the King. Our course

"We were given the third floor of the same building in which the Taif Government Dispensary had its quarters on the first floor. There were two doctors in Taif, the regular dispensary man and the surgeon, who had come from Mecca about three weeks before to look after the case for which we were called. Patients were few and far between, certainly not more than twenty-five daily. The Director of Health for Hedjaz arrived from Mecca the day after we did and remained there all the time. He was told by the King to find us a place to work and to prepare an operating room, which he did and did well. At once that dispensary was crowded with patients, the street was jammed, the hallway, the stairs and the corridors to our living rooms as well. This was a great surprise to me, for I had no idea that we would get any rush of patients. It did not take us very long to fill the ward space allowed us and we had to slow down.

"After remaining there a month I asked for permission to leave and this was granted. People had been coming from Jidda, Mecca, Medina and many smaller places. Many more inquiries were coming in asking about the length of our stay. When they learned we were leaving, a petition signed by about two hundred citizens was presented to the King asking him to have us stay at least another month. We promised another two weeks. When that was up some special friends of the King from Mecca sent him a telegram and a messenger asking that I be detained to treat some members of their family. After that I was detained some more because of the illness of the Amir of Jidda; and lastly I was detained several days in Riadh by telegraphic orders of the King to treat a member of his family there."

"We started our return journey on July 24th [1932], following the same route by which we had come...."

"On the evening of the twenty-sixth we camped outside the wall of Riadh and entered it early in the morning. Amir Faisal, second son of the King and governor of Hedjaz, was in Riadh, just having returned from his third European trip. He had returned via Angora, Teheran, Baghdad and Kuwait. He had not seen Riadh for seven years, having been in the Hedjaz since its capture. We had a very pleasant visit one evening...."

"We left Riadh on the morning of the thirtieth and arrived in Hofuf two days later. The following morning we started off for Ojeir and Bahrain, making the whole trip in nine hours. We had been away two months and thirteen days and had traveled nineteen hundred miles." ["A Trip to Taif", *Neglected Arabia*, Number 163, October-December 1932, pp. 7-15]

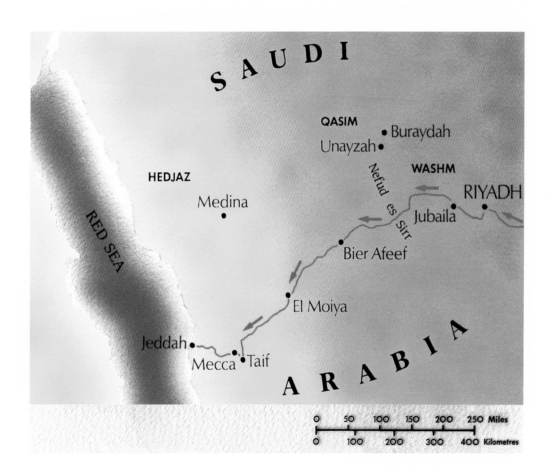

Dr Dame's route from Riyadh to Taif, 1932
[AMH]

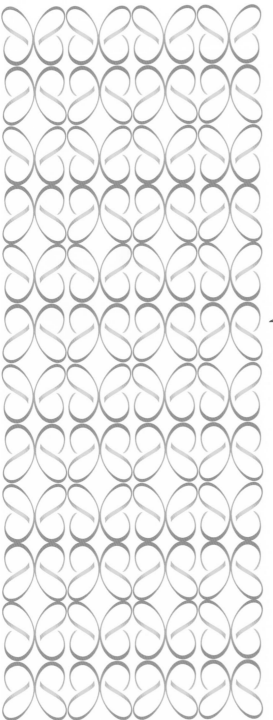

Chapter 8

A Son of the Pioneers

*T*he rocking of the ship had eased somewhat after rounding Budaiya and taking a southward course. Dr. Wells Thoms was glad his stomach was tolerating the sea passage better than Ibrahim's. His other assistant, Saroor, was an old hand at sailing having accompanied other doctors on similar trips. Wells had wanted to leave just after New Year's Day, 1937. However, a persistent *shamal* (north wind) had kept their ship moored at *Mina* Manama for the past five days. Now that the wind had abated, the medical team from Mason Memorial Hospital was able to comply with King Abdulaziz Al Saud's telegraphed request for Dr. Thoms to come to Riyadh.

Dr. Wells Thoms in the early 1930's.
[RCA]

The combined staff of the Bahrain Mission Hospitals in 1935
[AMH]

It was a sunny day with just enough breeze to create whitecaps on the open sea. The favorable wind took them quickly down the west coast of Bahrain past fishing villages and date gardens, then past the oil rigs surrounding *Jebel* Dukhan, the mountain in the middle of the island. It was clear that Bahrain, and probably the entire Gulf region was about to enter a new era.

The Captain of the ship-
sailing to Uqair in 1937
[RCA]

This sparsely populated corner of the earth where Wells' parents had come as missionary doctors in 1900, was now poised to generate more wealth from a black liquid under its soil than its inhabitants had ever been able to take in the form of pearls from the sea. Geologists working in Al-Hasa had told Wells about the half dozen test wells at *Jebel* Dhahran.

The ship turned due west from the barrenness of *Ras* Al-Bar, the cape at the south end of Bahrain, just as the afternoon sun began its descent. By

The customs pier at Uqair - the entry point to the Kingdom of Saudi Arabia [RCA]

sunset, all aboard were pleased to set their feet on the *terra firma* of the customs pier at Uqair. Zaki Effendi, the official in charge, greeted the medical team and took them to his home for supper, conversation and a night's rest. Accommodations were scarce in Uqair, so it was fortunate that Zaki was a friend. But the night was a short one, and the team was roused from sleep before dawn and sent off to Hofuf in a new Chevrolet automobile.

The car was equipped with wide, low-pressure tires. The drivers were experienced in negotiating the soft sand that covered much of the route between Uqair and Hofuf. The cars swerved back and forth to avoid sinking as they roared across the pale yellow dunes and past the unusual rock formations that marked the route inland. Not even two hours passed before the walls of Hofuf came into sight.

Dr. Thoms recalled his first view of this panorama just one month earlier. On that occasion, he had stopped his car on the rim of the basin in which Al-Hasa Oasis lay. He had taken several minutes to appreciate the magnitude of the gardens that stretched almost as far as the eye could see. From the midst of these gardens arose the

The market area adjacent to the walls of Hofuf in the 1930's.
[RCA]

The Governor of the Eastern province Abdulla ibn Jalawi [R] in the 1920's.
[RCA]

walls of Hofuf with towers and gates. With care, they had negotiated their way through the palms until they reached one of the city gates where they had left their cars in favor of walking to the palace of the governor. That visit was to be the only meeting Wells had with the famous Abdulla Ibn Jalawi.

Ibn Jalawi was, by that time, both very old and melancholy. His eldest son had died in battle years before. The father had never gotten over his grief. Wells had been led into the old man's *mejlis* and had offered a traditional greeting. The only response he had received was a wave of the old man's hand indicating where he should sit. After some minutes of absolute silence, Wells was greatly startled by the old man's voice shouting, *"gahwa"* (coffee). This shout had been picked up by the governor's retainers down the length of the room and across the courtyard to the kitchen where coffee was prepared.

That first visit to Hofuf had been occasioned by Ibn Jalawi's son, Sa'ad, who was suffering from trachoma and gradually losing his sight. Sa'ad had forwarded his request through the offices of Abdulrahman Al-Ghosaibi, whose family was prominent in the commerce of eastern Saudi Arabia, and who served as agents in Bahrain on behalf of King Abdulaziz Al Saud.

The offices of Abdulrahman Al-Ghosaibi's family business in Hofuf in the 1930's.
[RCA]

Dr. Thoms had been able to improve Sa'ad's vision and to relieve much of the discomfort he suffered with his eyes. In the course of that visit, Abdulrahman Al-Gosaibi had befriended Wells and had taken him to call on yet another prominent merchant in Hofuf, Mohammed Al-Ajaji.

This time, the team did not linger in Hofuf but was sent on toward Riyadh immediately. Saud Ibn Abdulla Ibn Jalawi was now the *Amir* of the Eastern Province and the one charged with facilitating the medical team's transit to Riyadh. A new truck was provided to carry the boxes of medical equipment and supplies, while a Ford touring car took their personal baggage. However, the car provided for Dr. Thoms and his two assistants was a rickety affair about which they were very uncertain. They allowed themselves to be driven three or four miles beyond Hofuf at which point they concluded that the car was not satisfactory and determined that they would return to *Amir* Saud and protest. Just then, the car stalled and would not restart. The *Amir* must have expected as much, because shortly thereafter one of his drivers came by in the new Chevrolet that had carried the team from Uqair to Hofuf. Back to Hofuf they went to see the *Amir*. He was reluctant to send them to Riyadh in his new Chevrolet automobile as he was looking forward to using it in the winter hunts. But he had no choice regarding the doctor and his companions, so off they went toward the capital in the *Amir's* Chevrolet.

Starting out again from Hofuf toward Riyadh, Dr. Thoms, Saroor and Ibrahim met up with their truck and touring car by *Ain Najem* (the Spring of the Star) where they took baths in the hot, sulfurous water. Such luxury was not available in Riyadh. An hour before sunset, the caravan headed west. Their travel was interrupted frequently by problems with the Ford touring car. All of the ignition wires had been spliced at one point or another, and various bits were held together by string. But the makeshift repairs they made early in the trip worked throughout the remainder, and by midnight they had reached Uray'irah. The oasis was abandoned at the time, so they cooked and ate their supper and rested for a couple of hours protected from the wind by an old mud-walled fort.

Well before dawn, the party set off again. At dawn, they paused at a spring to pray and fill water bags. At noon, they stopped for lunch at the edge of the Dahna sands. These were later crossed with only two or three interruptions to push the large truck out of soft sand. But it was midnight when they reached the gates of Riyadh, and these were shut. Only after the party persisted in making requests were the guards willing to rouse an official capable of deciding to open the gates and rescue the travelers from the cold winds blowing off the desert.

The following morning, Dr. Thoms, Saroor and Ibrahim went back out to the desert to await the King. From a low hill, Wells watched as distant dust clouds approached across the plain revealing phalanxes of cars driving ten abreast. These came screeching and skidding to a halt near the medical party and the King himself stepped out with Crown Prince Saud to receive the visitors. Wells could not help but be impressed by the manner and appearance of both King Abdulaziz and his son. They were invited to attend the King's *mejlis* that evening.

Dr. Thoms thought back to his first encounter with King Abdulaziz Al Saud less than a month ago. The King had visited Hofuf when Wells was there in December, and had asked to be fitted for reading glasses. This was easily done, but the King was disappointed to learn that it would require several weeks for his glasses to arrive from India. Moreover, the royal patient had surprised Dr. Thoms by requesting plastic instead of gold frames for his glasses. The less expensive plastic, it seemed, was more in keeping with *Wahabi* ethics. However, the King wanted a dozen pairs so that he could leave them in the several locations he frequented. The order had been placed with a request to expedite shipment via air mail.

King Abdulaziz Al-Saud with retainers
[RCA]

The primary purpose of this trip was to provide eye care to several members of the royal household. A number of the children and grandchildren suffered from trachoma and required medical and surgical treatment. Two girls, one a niece and the other a granddaughter of the King, were about fourteen years of age and would be marriageable except for their appearance. They each had one eye that was painful and unsightly due to chronic ulcers. Dr. Thoms removed the girls' diseased eyes and treated their wounds until they healed. Then he brought a selection of artificial eyes for the girls to try. In front of a mirror, they examined the possibilities. Dr. Thoms stepped out of their room briefly, and when he returned, he found that the King had come in and was quite indignant. It turned out that there was one blue eye among the many brown artificial eyes. The young women had found it and each tried it on. Both were quite taken with the idea of having one blue and one brown eye. Just as it appeared that a conflict was brewing, King Abdulaziz had entered the room and was admiring the girls' new look when he discerned the different colors of one girl's eyes. He was horrified and exclaimed that no one in their family had ever had blue eyes and that was not about to change. So conflict was averted and each girl contented herself with a new brown eye.

Regarding their medical work on behalf of the general public, Dr. Thoms later wrote:

"We work at the 'saheeyah,' a native house rudely adapted to the needs of a dispensary. One room contains our drugs and in it presides Ibraheem.... Saroor

presides in another room where he gives injections, pulls teeth, and sterilizes instruments and dressings for operations. I have a larger central room where I examine and treat patients. We fixed up another for our operating room, covering the windows and ceiling with gauze and hanging a petromax light over our touring operating table for illumination. By 'flitting' the room frequently as well as the patients when they enter we have kept the flies down to a minimum.

A young Arab
[RCA]

Now that all the royal family, as well as their servants have gone to al Khuffs we can devote our entire time to the needy populace. Our clinics are crowded from early morning to noon. After a hurried lunch we see a few special cases in their houses and then return to the 'sahiyah' for operating. Today we performed thirty eye operations, starting at four p.m. and finishing the last case at eleven. The Lord has blessed our work and our results are better than we had dared to hope for. Two of the cases which got the best results are religious leaders here. They were almost stone blind and now they can see well enough to read large print, and are overjoyed that they can read their Koran again....

"Medically, the prestige of the mission is high. We are thanked cordially for what we do, by merchant, priest, prince and pauper....

"Our stay in Riadh is drawing to an end. We hope to see the king today when he returns from al Khuffs and ask his permission to return to Bahrain. He will be leaving for Mecca in a few days. He must be there for the Hajj since he is the guardian of the holy cities. We have had a pleasant and successful tour. We have made many friends and have treated thousands. Our operations total more than three hundred. We have had the privilege of being used by God to help restore their sight to scores of blind people. There are few experiences more thrilling than that of watching a patient's face light up with joy when his bandages are removed after a cataract operation and he finds he can see once more." ["From a Doctor's Journal", *Neglected Arabia*, Number 180, October-December 1937, pp. 12-13]

*Oil - "an important new
industry at Bahrain"
in the 1930's
[RCA]*

*A traditional
sailing ship in the
Arabian Gulf
[RCA]*

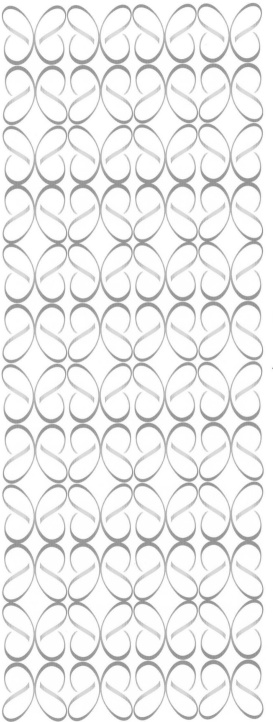

Chapter 9

*Lady Practitioners
for Lady
Patients*

Josephine Van Peursem

Josephine Van Peursem was glad to have two Indian nurses working alongside her and looked forward to the arrival of two more. She had been in charge of the Marion Wells Thoms Memorial Hospital since Dr. Tiffany's departure in June. The worldwide economic depression might have slowed down other activities, but not the hospitals. By mid-year, it appeared that the Bahrain hospitals would set new records in 1933. She felt stretched in her role and was thankful for the support of Dr. Dame and the newly arrived Dr. Wells Thoms.

It was now 23 years since she had been appointed to serve as a nurse in the American Mission. She had begun her career in Bahrain studying Arabic. Shortly thereafter, she had married Gerrit Van Peursem, another of the appointees of 1910. While her training for the nursing profession had been quite thorough, her experiences on the job in the various stations of the American Mission had forced her to learn many additional skills.

One of those experiences had come in 1914 when Dr. Paul Harrison had asked Josephine to accompany him on his second trip to Qatif. The local *shaikh* had requested a "lady doctor" to treat some female members of his household. Most of the time, Josephine had worked independently caring not only for the *shaikhaat*, but also for other members of their household, their friends, and women of other households. Very few ladies would come to the clinic, and Josephine had spent her days being taken from house to house applying her skills to the complete range of ailments prevalent in Qatif.

Now there were to be new experiences and new challenges. Dr. Louis Dame had received another invitation, actually an urgent request, from King Abdulaziz Al Saud to bring a medical team to Riyadh. This invitation added the specific request for a *"hakima"* (lady doctor) or a nurse. After hurried preparations, the party set out from Bahrain and sailed to Uqair on July 26th. Mrs. Dame wrote:

"The journey was made in three laps, by launch from Bahrain to Ojeir, by motor from Ojeir to El Hofhuf, where we rested until the motor convoy was ready to convey us from El Hofhuf to Riadh.

Market place adjacent to the city walls of Hofuf in the 1930's.
[RCA]

This convoy consisted of two touring cars and three lorries, all of which were packed like sardines with people, bedding, tents, luggage, petrol, water and various odds and ends. We even had a live sheep in one of the lorries -- our meat supply -- on the hoof, you see.

"The desert between Ojeir and El Hofhuf is mostly undulating sand dunes with a stretch of salt pans in the middle. The sand dunes are fairly high and beautifully rounded and are made of luscious yellow sand, so pure and clean looking. One of the marvels of the trip was the ease with which the motors glided up and over these dunes which one might easily imagine well-nigh impassable. It was an unusual but splendid 'whoopee' ride.

"The sand dunes finish to the east of El Hofhuf and the desert on the other side presents a variety of topography. One crosses plain hard rocky levels, stretches of soft sand where cars get stuck and in general there is a gradual rise as one climbs up to the Nejd Plateau, Riadh having an altitude of 2000 feet. We took a

Dr. & Mrs. Dame in Arabic dress during a visit to Hofuf in the 1930's.
[RCA]

semicircular sweep or horseshoe curve from El Hofhuf, going northwest, then west, then southwest, to avoid the sand dunes of the Dahna. The camel caravans take a more direct east and west route.

"Our general plan of travel was to get up early and ride until an hour or so before noon, when a campsite would be reached, preferably near a well and there we would pitch our tents and rest for a few hours in the heat of the day and have our midday meal. Then in the afternoon we would break camp and ride on until late in the evening when we would stop, unroll our bedding and go to sleep under the stars on our beds of sand.

Ladies resting by the cars during a desert crossing
[RCA]

"We were travelling at the end of July at the season of the very worst heat. The desert was parched, not a green thing growing. We learned how terrible thirst can be. Our precious skins of water had to last between wells for there were long stretches where absolutely not a drop was procurable. There are only three wells between El Hofhuf and Riadh. And oh! How thirsty we got. We drank often but all the membranes of our noses, mouths and throats were as dry as dust and we never really seemed able to quench our burning thirst. Some of the water we *drank too was anything but choice, being neither clean nor appetizing, but it was wet and that was the prime requisite. One cannot be finicky on a tour!"*

A medical convoy stopped en route to Riyadh
[RCA]

We spent three nights on the desert, which cooled off considerably compared to the daytime heat. Early in the morning the Delil (guide) would arouse the caravan by calling, "Yalla! gumu!" (O God! hurry, rise). It was anything but a welcome sound, so very early in the morning, before daylight, the air still chilly and our blankets snug and warm. But it was a summons that had to be obeyed and we made short work of dressing, rolling up our bedding, gulping down some strong tea or bitter Arab coffee, into the cars and off before we were fairly awake. We covered many miles before sun-up, but had our reward in seeing the majesty of the sunrise over the spacious desert sands. It was not long after the sunrise however when the day's heat began to be felt.

"Our third camping site was in a little valley between rocky hills (like Muscat) where acacia trees grew and a few pungent herbs. It was nice to see some vegetation once more.

"The last stretch was a mad race to reach Riadh before sunset. Most of you have experienced that 'so near and yet so far' feeling. The cars of the convoy, realizing that the need for keeping together for mutual protection and assistance had passed, set out each for himself, to make the goal. Finally, we came in sight of the palm trees -- the gardens on the outskirts of the city -- and then the city walls themselves in the distance. We stopped at a garden called 'Shemsia' where fresh water was brought to us and we drank it greedily by the quart. Surely, water never tasted so good before.

"Then we went on more leisurely to the city's gate. Riadh has a medieval appearance with its walls, turrets and crenellated roofs. We entered one of the main gates, which was just wide enough to let the car through. On either side stood armed guards. The car eased through the gate and we were riding down the

Sand dunes in the Dahna Sands east of Riyadh
[PLA]

main street. A thrill passed through us. We had arrived in Riadh, the capital city of Nejd!" ["A Trip to Central Arabia", *Neglected Arabia*, Number 167, January-March 1934, pp. 5-8]

The medical convoy
entering Riyadh
[RCA]

Josephine Van Peursem, Elizabeth Dame and their female companions from Bahrain were given half of a house belonging to the King's brother. After making some adjustments, they were able to settle down to life in Riyadh. It took several more days to become accustomed to the perpetual squeaking of pulleys over nearby wells as water was brought to the surface.

Mrs. Van Peursem's work as a nurse was greatly appreciated in the royal household. On Fridays in the afternoon, the ladies from Bahrain were invited to the *mejlis* where King Abdulaziz met with his women relatives. Mrs. Dame related the following conversation:

The house belonging to the King's brother, used by the ladies of the medical team in Riyadh
[RCA]

"On this day after he had greeted the assembly and settled himself on the cushions he looked over at the foreign ladies in their Arab costumes and asked me, 'Sahala, when you get back to your country will you wear those clothes?'

"I replied, 'Yes, occasionally.'"

"He said, 'Oh, of course. You will wear them to dances.'"

"I responded that I was not in the habit of going to dances and he exclaimed,

Elizabeth Dame and Josephine Van Peursem "at home" in Riyadh [RCA]

'Why, all Americans go to dances.'"

"I calmly assured him that all of them did not go for I did not go."

"Then he said, 'Certainly that is right. You two are mutedayyineen (religious) and the mutedayyineen do not go to dances.' Then turning to the company he explained carefully that we were good people and religious and we were called mubeshereen (missionaries) and that we spent our lives in service for the sake of our religion. It sounded so much nicer in Arabic than it does in English and it was a tribute we appreciated very much. It also showed that the King knows where we stand and that we were not sailing under any false colors."

"Our greatest interest of course was in the women. We found them very responsive and were met with friendliness and cordiality on every hand, whether from members of the royal family, wives of retainers, servants or slaves. We felt when we left that we were leaving real friends, for our intimate association had deepened our acquaintanceship to friendship even in the short space of three months.

"We often thanked our lucky stars that we had had many years of experience in our basic stations in Arabia before this trip to the interior. The proper requisite for such a trip is most assuredly many years of contact and experience with Arabs and fluency in Arabic. It flattened all obstacles and smoothed our way tremendously. The women later admitted that they had had grave misgivings when they knew we were coming. They did not know what to expect and evidently were pleasantly surprised. I think our Arab dress, knowledge of Arabic and Arab ways combined with the fortunate circumstances of our both having brown eyes and dark hair and of not being too thin (!) disarmed any preconceived prejudices they might have had and we got off to an even start. Then as soon as Mrs. Van

Peursem began on her medical work the race was as good as won."

"The object of the trip to Nejd was the medical treatment of two ladies of the King's household. Both of them were operated upon by Dr. Dame and nursed with consummate skill and tenderness by Mrs. Van Peursem, ably assisted by Nurse Grace. The operations were performed in the country castle, "Bedia," some nine kilometers from Riadh. The first operation was the more difficult and entailed constant after care so we moved out to Bedia and lived there for two weeks, which gave us a real insight into the running of a Moslem home and of a royal household in particular. The peach orchard was at its prime then and we enjoyed our occasional excursions to it.

"When the second operation was performed and that patient was settled in our wing of the castle with her children, servants and slaves, we moved back to our town house and made daily visits, often spending the whole day. One morning when Mrs. Van Peursem walked into this patient's room she encountered a little old Bedouiya [Bedouin woman]. *The two stopped and stared at*

Louis Dame, Harold Storm [standing]
Rob Roy Storm and Elizabeth Dame [seated]
[RCA]

each other a moment incredulously. 'Why,' exclaimed Mrs. Van Peursem, 'aren't you Um Nura?' (mother of Nura).

"'Yes,' excitedly replied the little desert woman, 'and you are no other than Khatoon Lateefa, Um Lulu.' (mother of Pearl).

"The American missionary nurse and the little Arab woman had met again, after a period of nineteen years. Um Nura at that time had been in the Bahrain hospital with her sick daughter and now after these many years they met and recognized each other in Central Arabia. To me it was one of the high lights of the trip and an incident of great significance.

"In the future there will be many women and children who will remember this visit, for Um Lulu became very popular. With her skill and kind and gentle manner combined with her patience and readiness to listen to all their complaints she soon had as much work as could be crowded into a day. With the two special operative patients to look after and a number of other special patients who received almost daily treatments in their own homes, there was no time for a regular clinic even if there had been a suitable place provided and there was none such at the very inadequate building which passed for the Men's Hospital. But wherever she went, after the special patient had been treated, as though at a given signal, a dispensary would be suddenly in full swing as friends, servants and slaves of the hostess would crowd in bringing their children with all sorts of troubles and illnesses. It was seldom that twenty or twenty-five extra persons were not treated daily in this way." ["A Trip to Central Arabia", *Neglected Arabia*, Number 167, January-March 1934, pp. 16-21]

Josephine Van Peursem summarized her experience for the Annual Report of 1933:

"The work among the women of Riadh was as much of a social interest as it was of health value. In our visits with the women we did concentrate on health talks, hygiene and infant care....

Dr. Paul Harrison and an Arab patient in Riyadh, 1935.
[RCA]

"Whenever and wherever we visited, the circle of women present soon turned into a small dispensary. Several of the royal ladies received regular treatments and after these were over, as if by signal, relatives with children, slaves and their little ones would appear by dozens, needing quinine, mixtures, eye-drops, ointments, etc. We treated approximately twenty-five patients a day among the women." ["Annual Report-1934", *Neglected Arabia*, Number 168, April-June 1934, p. 14]

Josephine had an opportunity to revisit her friends in central Arabia just a few months later in the winter of 1935. Mrs. Dame wrote in a "round robin" letter that circulated among the various stations of the American Mission:

The travelling medical team from Bahrain, 1935 [RCA]

"As most of you know the station personnel was depleted by the departure of the whole Van Peursem family and Dr. Dame plus an Indian nurse and several helpers of both sexes on Feb. 18th when the party set sail for Ojair en route for Nejd. News from the party indicates that they had a pleasant voyage to Ojair, where the populace lined up for medical attention; then a quick motor trip to El Hofhuf where a busy two days were spent in both social and professional calls; then a fairly good trip to the great encampment 'El Khuffs' where the King and his family were enjoying a 'next to nature' sort of glorified picnic. The wide wady was covered with multicolored flowers; meadowlarks sang around the tents; everything was lovely except when the sand blew down from the nearby dunes. A few days of this ease, with occasional teas and dinners with Mr. Philby, and a day of hunting and then Dr. Dame and Bobby [Van Peursem] *went to Riadh to unpack and get settled. Mrs. Van* [Peursem] *stayed to treat women of the royal harem until their departure for the Haj. Then the Van* [Peursem]*'s also sought Riadh. There*

they have been busy with clinics, operations and outcalls." ["Bahrain Round Robin" letter dated March 30, 1935]

Later in the same trip, April 8th, 1935, to be exact, Mr. Van Peursem wrote a letter from Riyadh to a colleague in Kuwait:

"Mr. [Harry St. John] Philby dropped in yesterday, and he consented to take some mail for us to Kuweit. So we are sending our greetings with them. In the afternoon Mr. Ph[ilby] drove us in his new 8 cyl[inder] 7 seater Ford to some of the gardens. And then after some visiting with Arabs they had dinner with us. It was exceedingly interesting to have had this visit. Mrs. Ph[ilby] looked quite charming in her new Arab outfit that the king had given her. As you know all our women veil here and Mrs. Ph[ilby] too but they pull it aside as soon as they are away from the Arabs. Mr. Ph[ilby] told us the details of the attempt on the king's life. He told us much that we had not heard here. Both Mr. & Mrs. Ph[ilby] are driving all the way to London. With that nice car of theirs it will not be much of a hardship. I hope you will have a chance to visit with them while they are in Kuweit. They can tell you how we are situated here.

"Our program is this: leave Riyadh on 15 Apr for Hail. The medical people hope to carry on there for 21 days and then come south as far as Barada and do the same thing there for 21 days. That will bring us back to Riyadh by about Rubia al Awal. Chances are that we will not be in Bahrain before Rubia Al Thani. Dr. Dame says it is no use staying in a place less than 21 days for then one cannot operate, for there is not enough time for patients to recover before we leave.

*Medical convoy
entering Hail in 1935
[RCA]*

He and Josephine have about 300 patients every day except Sundays. It has been hard on my wife to walk to and from the hospital. All the cars have been to Mecca. Only now do we have a car at our disposal, but our time is almost up." [Letter from G. W. Van Peursem to Fred Barny dated "Riyadh. April 8-35"]

*Patients waiting to
be seen in Hail, 1935
[RCA]*

In yet another letter, Mr. Van Peursem wrote:

"The missionary party remained in Riyadh, the capital of Nejd, five weeks. The doctor and his assistants were kept very busy. Every morning about two hundred men and the same number of women appeared for treatment. This dispensary work was usually over by 1:30 p.m. The afternoons were devoted to operations. On some days the doctor was still operating at 8:00 in the evening. Often he was so busy that he just had to send men away. The king and his household were in Mecca; so the poor people had an opportunity to get medical attention." ["Into the Heart of Arabia", *The Church Herald,* July 10, 1935; p. 28]

In the winter months of 1943, Josephine Van Peursem accompanied Dr. Esther Barny to Riyadh for what was to be her final visit to inland Arabia. In 1946, she and her husband returned to the United States and retired. Their trips into the Kingdom of Saudi Arabia remained among their fondest memories.

The mission medical team enjoying a meal in Hail, 1935 [RCA]

Dr. Esther Barny

Dr. Esther
[RCA]

Dr. Esther Barney inspected the Mason Memorial Hospital as she walked toward it. The play of light and shadow created by the setting sun accented the arches and lintels that were its dominant architectural features. It was a grand building done in the local style with broad verandahs on all sides. But as she approached it, she could see the sags and cracks that were beginning to appear in its fabric. The cornerstone of the hospital had been laid in March of 1902, the same month in which she had been born to missionary parents in Basrah, Iraq. At 36, she was glad that time was treating her more kindly than the hospital building.

Dr. Harold Storm had sent a messenger across the mission compound to summon Esther from the Marion Wells Thoms Memorial Hospital where she cared for women patients and their infants. It was tiring work. She was the only woman physician in Bahrain. She had been back in station for a year and a half, and the workload had been heavy and constant. Usually she was the one who summoned Dr. Storm when she needed another surgeon to assist with a procedure on one of her lady patients. As her long legs carried her through the door of the men's hospital, she wondered what her colleague had in mind.

*Dr. Esther Barny and Indian nurses from the
staff of the women's hospital in Bahrain.*
[RCA]

Harold Storm was completing his surgical notes for the afternoon. He greeted the tall Esther with his usual, "Hi, Shorty," and motioned to her to sit in a chair at the table where he was writing. After adding a few last lines, he capped his pen and looked at her with a wry smile.

He picked up a cabled message that had been delivered to the hospital several minutes before. He pretended to read and reread it affecting a great deal of seriousness.

"OK, Harold," said Esther. "It's so unusual for you to be struck dumb. Give it to me if you won't tell me what it says."

"Well," Harold began. "It's from Dr. Dame. It seems that the King would like our esteemed colleague to bring a lady doctor to his capital. Louis wants to know when you'll arrive in Qatif."

After crossing the water to Qatif, Esther was met by representatives of CASOC with a truck and a car. Her baggage was loaded and she was driven along the hardened track leading to the oil camp. Here she joined the Dames and spent the night. Then, together with the Dames, she set off the following morning toward Riyadh via Hofuf. At first it was like an amusement park ride--rushing up the sides of sand dunes wondering if the car would launch into space, then down the opposite slope. The drivers obviously knew their business. There were few stops to dislodge a car or truck bogged down in soft sand. Much of the route was over hard desert surfaces and the trip passed quickly, not at all like the days of travel on camelback that Dr. Dame had described to her.

Unfortunately, it seems that no one in Riyadh had anticipated Dr. Barny's arrival or made any plans regarding her activities. She later reported:

"One of the most interesting and enjoyable events of the year was my trip to Riadh. I had little opportunity for work in the town but from what I did see I could appreciate the appalling need. I hope that this trip will be a forerunner of many more to the interior." ["Annual Report-1938", *Neglected Arabia,* Number 185, April-June 1939, p. 8]

Indeed it was. Another invitation followed in the summer of 1939. With Dr. Dame, she planned for a two-month stay and packed accordingly. On August 10th, she made the steamy passage from Bahrain to the Arabian coast. That first night, Esther was accommodated in an air-conditioned house in the Dhahran camp. Two days later found the medical team situated in more traditional accommodations in Riyadh. King Abdulaziz was, as ever, a most gracious host and provided every opportunity for the lady doctor to care for the women of the palace and the town. Dr. Barny's planned two-month stay was extended to four during which time she saw hundreds of patients. She departed with a standing invitation from the King to return every year.

Dr. Barny made five more trips to Riyadh. Reflecting on her experiences she wrote:

"In 1942 a tour was made to Riadh with Dr. and Mrs. Harrison. It was a hard trip because of the heat of August and the intervening of the fast month. I was not too well. However, I renewed acquaintances in the King's family and treated swarms of women who poured into the clinic. I also ran a clinic in the King's palace for the slaves who needed treatment. Last year the King again sent for me, especially for one of the queens. Then early this present year Bin Saoud again sent. I lived in town in a new Arab house, which is quite comfortable. I mostly visited the women in their homes, spending the morning out at the palace and the afternoon in town. It is not a very satisfactory way of doing medicine but these women are extremely conservative and do not go out of their homes. The King wants me to come in for a month every six months as a standing order and be the official doctor of the palace women." ["Annual Report-1943", *Neglected Arabia*, Number 202, January-June 1944, p. 6]

Harold Storm has left us some further details regarding one of Dr. Barny's excursions to Riyadh. In the winter months of 1943, Dr. Storm was visiting

Riyadh per the request of King Abdulaziz. The King asked that Dr. Esther Barny come and treat some women of the royal family. In response to Dr. Storm's cabled inquiry, Dr. Harrison wired back that Dr. Barny was busy treating members of the royal family in Bahrain. Harold Storm wondered how he should break this news to the King. However, when Harold called on King Abdulaziz, he discovered that the King was already aware of Dr. Harrison's cabled message and was in a rage. The best Dr. Storm could do was offer to intervene on the King's behalf. However, the next communication from Dr. Harrison indicated that Dr. Barny had decided to come to Riyadh, which news was enough to satisfy to the King.

Esther Barny married Mr. John Ames of the Standard Oil Company on May 8, 1943. In addition to her responsibilities at the Marion Wells Thoms Memorial Hospital, she supervised the new Sulmaniya Hospital for women opened by the Government of Bahrain. Her tours into the Kingdom of Saudi Arabia were an addition to these two jobs. She is remembered as a quiet, cheerful person who thrived on her work and possessed great skill as a physician and surgeon. Her departure from Bahrain in 1945 was deeply regretted by the members of the American Mission, the women of Bahrain, and many more women in Saudi Arabia.

Dr. Louis & Elizabeth Dame in
the late 1930's
[ANS]

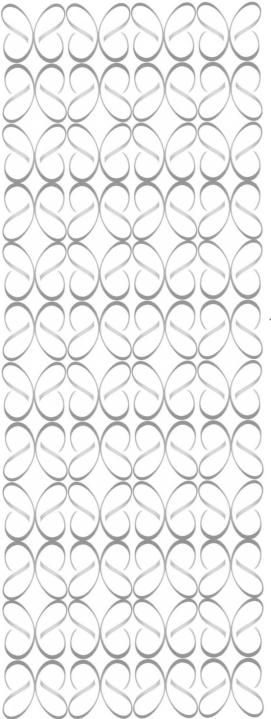

Chapter 10

*A Doctor
Treats the
Crown Prince*

A paragraph from the 1929 Annual Report of the American Mission reads:

> *"In Bahrein the outstanding feature of the year was the touring done by Dr. Dame -- two months on the Trucial coast and one in Hassa. Four invitations were received to visit Hassa. One of these was to treat Amir Saoud, oldest son of King Ibn Saoud and heir to the throne, a most gracious host and a frank, charming personality. Another was to treat the Governor of Hassa* [Ibn Jalawi], *who was suffering from melancholia after the death of his son in a battle with some rebel Bedouins. On the last trip to Hassa, Dr. Dame was for the first time allowed to treat the public."* ["Annual Report-1929", *Neglected Arabia*, Number 152, January-March 1930, p. 11]

As the years passed, Dr. Dame continued to have occasional contact with the Crown Prince, experiences he evidently enjoyed. Apart from the stop-off in Riyadh on the way to Taif in 1932, Dr. Dame made several more trips into the Kingdom and, no doubt, met with Crown Prince Saud during these visits. In 1933, the medical team from Mason Memorial Hospital spent three months in Riyadh. We have less detail about the 1934 tour, but in 1935, Dr. Dame's group spent six months between Riyadh and Hail. On this occasion, Dr. Paul Harrison participated once again after a lapse of eighteen years. Dr. Wells Thoms had joined the staff of the Mason Memorial Hospital by that time and began touring in Al-Hasa and later in Riyadh. Each of them had the pleasure of encountering the Crown Prince.

In December 1937, Prince Saud Ibn Abdulaziz Al Saud visited Bahrain as a guest of the *Amir* of Bahrain, *Shaikh* Hamad bin Isa Al-Khalifa. A great deal of celebration accompanied this visit and the Crown Prince was taken to see various sites around the island. At the request of Crown Prince Saud, the royal party visited the hospitals of the American Mission. In a letter written by Gerrit Van Peursem to his supervisor in New York, he said:

Crown Prince Saud ibn Abdulaziz Al-Saud
with the Amir of Bahrain,
Shaikh Hamad bin Isa Al Khalifa
[RCA]

"The visit of Amir Sa'ud of Arabia to Bahrain in December was a grand success. He with his retinue, occupied the sheikh's palace. They remained ten days in Bahrain. The amir had a very busy program. Every single community desired to show him honor. The amir was kind enough to come to the mission for tea one Sunday afternoon. The ruling sheikh also honored us with his presence that afternoon. It was a very appropriate time, we felt, to make the amir acquainted with all the members of the station. We hope that this helped to make the bond of friendship between the mission and the Sa'udi government all the stronger. The missionaries had an opportunity of visiting with the amir and his brothers at dinners given by the British and prominent Arabs in honor of the noted guest. I do not think that our sheikh has ever entertained more lavishly." [Letter from G. W. Van Peursem to Dr. Potter dated January 27, 1938]

Shaikh Hamad Bin Isa Al-Khalifa, the Amir of Bahrain in 1937
[RCA]

The Shaikh Hamad palace as it appeared during the state visit of Crown Prince Saud to Bahrain, 1937
[RCA]

Shaikh Hamad bin Isa Al-Khalifa and his son Shaikh Sulman, with other Arab men in 1937
[RCA]

Like his father in 1923, a day came when Crown Prince Saud Ibn Abdulaziz needed the services of Dr. Dame above all others. While the Crown Prince's life was not in immediate danger, the welfare of one of his limbs was. In a letter written in Riyadh, Dr. Dame passed the details of this episode to his colleague Dr. Mylrea in Kuwait.

"Riadh, November 2, 1939"

"Dear Mylrea:

"On October 7th there was an 'Ardha' or open air display with sword dancing and so on, to celebrate the completion of reading the Koran by one of the King's sons, besides one or two of his nephews. The usual dancing was going on in the square in front of the town castle.

Arab men performing a traditional dance in Riyadh in the 1930's. [RCA]

When the display was over the young princes with some of their retainers went outside the city wall on horseback and there was the usual shouting and galloping. This had just come to an end and the Crown Prince Sa'ud was raising himself in the saddle to dismount when another horse came into collision with Sa'ud's horse. Sa'ud lost his balance and fell, with the result that he sustained a supra condylar and condylar T comminuted fracture of the humerus of the left arm.

"I was only a short distance away when it happened but did not actually see the accident. I overheard a bystander say, 'Someone has fallen off his horse. It's the Amir Sa'ud!' Several of his brothers bundled him into a car, and started down the street. They had only just got under way when they saw me. I boarded their car suggesting that we go to the X-ray plant. This was done and the X-ray man (he is very good) came as did two of the doctors who are on the King's staff. Together we set Sa'ud's arm, which was not as easy an operation as it may sound.

"The X-ray plant is a very good Siemens outfit but there is no hospital connected with it and of course nothing with which to immobilize a fracture. Fortunately I had some excellent Johnson and Johnson plaster splints and rolls at my place. These I fetched, together with everything else I needed or thought I needed.

"We were just ready to begin our plaster work when the King came storming in. He was furious because he had not been informed immediately and sent three of his sons off to jail as a punishment. Then he wanted to know how we were going to treat the broken bone. I told him that we were going to set it in plaster and showed him our paraphernalia. The King spurned them and said that was no way to put up a broken arm. What it needed was tight wooden splints, he added. Then he sent for the official bone-setter, who is also a well known builder in Riadh. At the same time he continued to lecture us doctors on the art of bone-setting and splinting. We did not pay much attention but quietly adjusted the plaster splints.

"I retorted at one point that plaster was used the world over for fractures, except in Riadh, and that Qubba the mason perhaps knew his clay, although at that he *couldn't even build his walls straight, and that he had better stick to his building and leave broken bones alone. When presently Bin Qubba did arrive in the X-ray room, we were checking the fracture in the hardening plaster. He came to look at it, but said,*

'Where is it? I don't see it.'

"The King was quieter now and I softly whispered to Bin Qubba,

'It's all finished now. Your services are not needed.'

"The Amir Muhammad Bin Abdur Rahman now came in, as well as any number of other members of the royal family. They were so numerous that we could hardly get around. The Amir, having inspected our work, proceeded to give his opinion. 'The broken bones will never unite, never, never, never. Only if we use the well-tried Arab procedure will we have a satisfactory result.'

"During the next few days, there was a tremendous lot of disapproval expressed of our new method of setting fractures.

Dr. Esther Barny was able to get the reaction of the women, especially in the palace. When after three days we had to loosen the cast because of swelling, it was nip and tuck whether the case would be taken away from us or not. We wanted to put the arm in a new cast but we also wanted to wait until the swelling had subsided. A morning had been set for the job, but when I saw that there still remained some swelling I refused to do it that day.

"The other doctors then said that the King

Dr. Louis Dame travelling in the deserts of Arabia
[RCA]

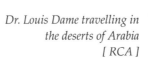

had ordered it done that day and would be extremely angry if it was not done. We therefore drove to the Murabba and I explained to the King the necessity for waiting till the swelling had subsided. He was very courteous and said,

'Very well, do as you please. Whatever you think ought to be done go ahead and do it.' So that was that.

"Two weeks later when the cast became a bit loose we just changed it without asking permission. That drew a broadside from the King. Two of the King's doctors were having dinner with us that evening and we had just sat down to the table when a messenger arrived. The King wanted Dr. Rashad at the Murabba at once. The telephone operator had been told that if he did not get Dr. Rashad to the Murabba within ten minutes, the King would have him put to death. Very naturally the operator implored Dr. Rashad to go at once. He did, in a borrowed car.

"When he got to the palace the King lit into him about changing the plaster without consulting him. The King also dilated at some length on the whole question of plaster treatment for broken bones. The result was that Dr. Rashad sent in his resignation after a day or two. (All that has been settled, however, and Dr. Rashad's wife and baby have just arrived from Jidda).

"At this juncture we again almost lost the case. Muhammad Bin Abdur Rahman called on Sa'ud the next morning and a little later I was sent for. There sat the King's three doctors consulting together by themselves, pictures of dejection. They said that Sa'ud had told them that he thought it would be best to have the cast removed and then have the arm set in the Arab way. I had been in to see Sa'ud

The Murabba, the palace of King Abdulaziz Al-Saud in Riyadh in the 1930's
[RCA]

early that day because I had some operations on my list. Otherwise we doctors usually came at about the same time and saw the patient together.

"When I left, Muhammad Bin Abdur Rahman came in, and since he had been one of our chief opponents all through the business, I am pretty sure that it was he who persuaded Sa'ud that modern doctors know nothing about fractures.

"However we doctors went in, examined the cast and declared that everything was satisfactory. I then proceeded to explain that all the world over, the plaster cast was the favorite treatment for fractures. I told how I had spent two months of my last leave in fracture wards and had taken a special course. I told about Cook County Hospital in Chicago with its three wards of sixty beds each, for fractures only. I promised to produce two new books on fractures which just a few days before had reached me, forwarded from Bahrain. That afternoon I went to see Sa'ud again bringing not two but three books, on fractures - Bohler of Vienna, Key and Connel, and a book on industrial surgery. I took particular pains to show him the pictures especially those of casts on arms. He was greatly interested and spoke a lot about the hospitals he had seen in London.

"November 8, 1939

"Still in Riadh, but I haven't done anything the past week. I have been down in bed with a bad cold and fever rising to 104°. However, yesterday my temperature remained normal all the twenty-four hours, so today I called on the Amir Sa'ud, my first stepping out. Tomorrow we take off the cast.

"I think we have got a pretty good result, though when the cast comes off and he tries to bend the elbow we can tell better. The condyles were broken in four places. One crack ran directly into the joint. We obtained a good apposition in these. The shaft did not come into perfect alignment but I am more than hopeful for a good functional result.

"There is no doubt that Riadh, or any other place in Nejd is a surgeon's paradise. We have had just all that we could do. The fact that the total figures for our three months stay are not very large is due to the fact that our last month was given almost entirely to Sa'ud. At the time of his accident we had just about exhausted our hospital supplies. Once having stopped surgery, except for emergency cases, we did not start again. Even so we performed about one hundred and forty surgical operations."

"Sincerely yours,

(Signed) L. P. Dame

"P. S. November 12, 1939

"I have not yet had an opportunity to send this letter to Kuwait so I can report on the progress of Sa'ud's arm. We took it out of the cast three days ago and had him do some active motion. This he does quite freely and can now flex the elbow to about ninety degrees, which we think quite good. His arm is now in a wire basket splint. We remove it from this splint twice daily and keep the elbow joint gently moving. Everybody is happy about the outcome and I need not say that we doctors are elated. It has been proved to Riadh and to the hard-boiled sceptics that western doctors do know something about treating fractures, and that methods other than those of the Nejd, do work. And I am just conceited enough to believe that but for my presence the arm would have been turned over to a local bone-setter, with a stiff arm for life as a result.

"I must get this off now. Dhahran is sending four cars for us - one sedan, two station wagons, and one truck. Once more goodbye and best wishes to you all.

"Sincerely,

(Signed) L. P. Dame"
[*Kuwait Before Oil* -- the memoirs of Dr. C. Stanley G. Mylrea (unpublished), 1951, pp. 155-161]

Chapter 11

*Another Doctor
More Tours*

Dr. Harold Storm enjoyed the smell of diesel fumes and the throbbing of the boat's engine. This was a much better way to travel than in the old days when one depended on the winds. Even though the deck of the boat was crowded, he found paths on which to pace back and forth, as if by much walking he would hasten their arrival. Harold was not a patient man. He would have been pleased if he could have boarded an airplane for the trip from Bahrain to Hofuf, but no such regular service existed in 1944.

Crossing from Bahrain to Uqair en route to Al-Hasa [RCA]

The World War had made it difficult to obtain supplies for the hospitals in Bahrain. As a result, the plan for this tour was to concentrate on surgical cases, especially eyes, as this was Harold's *forte.* Harold was a surgeon at heart, so this state of affairs was not particularly disturbing to him. He knew there were plenty of surgical cases needing attention in the region of Al-Hasa.

The brother of the Provincial Governor or *Amir* had occasioned this trip, and the services of the team could not be extended to others until this man, Abdulaziz Ibn Jalawi, had undergone surgery. A makeshift operating room was prepared in the palace. The procedure did not begin well as the tray of materials for administering the spinal anesthetic proved defective. Harold worried that the patient might give up before Abdulnabi could bring another tray from the house where they were staying. In fact, the patient was very cooperative, and

Abdulnabi Sabkar dispensing pharmaceuticals at Mason Memorial Hospital
[ANS]

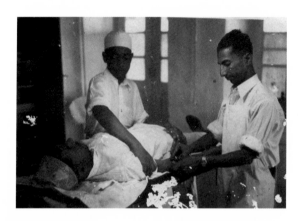

*Abdulnabi Sabkar
treating a patient
[ANS]*

*Abdulnabi Sabkar with his bicycle in
front of Mason Memorial Hospital
[ANS]*

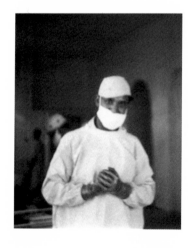

*Abdulnabi Sabkar
scrubbed for surgery
[ANS]*

his surgery, although complex, went well. But several hours following the operation, the patient suffered from a severe headache, fever and vomiting. Harold suspected that this was a reaction to the spinal anesthetic, and fortunately it resolved quickly.

Harold called on the *Amir* almost every day. On one occasion, he found the Governor in bed near a blazing fire covered with blankets and rugs. Harold, lightly dressed, immediately began to perspire in the heat of the room. The *Amir,* like most of his subjects, suffered from bouts of malaria.

Unfortunately, shifting sand dunes often prevented the ample waters of Al-Hasa Oasis from reaching the sea. Instead, the springs flowed into pools and irrigation ditches. These extensive bodies of still water provided excellent breeding

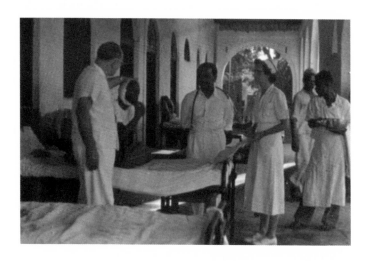

Dr. Harold Storm making rounds among the patients on the verandah of Mason Memorial Hospital [AMH]

grounds for the anopheles mosquito, so malaria was endemic in the region.

It took some time to obtain a place where the team could set up a temporary hospital. Harold worried that the staff, in the meantime, was having too much fun in this slack period. They were swimming, horseback riding and visiting the bazaar on a daily basis. However, a house was found for them and they set it up to serve their purposes. It took some time to get satisfactory floor coverings, fabric for flyscreens and mosquito netting. But when all was ready, the patients came and everyone worked hard.

On the first day, they saw seventy-one patients and performed eleven operations. One was a tonsillectomy for a patient who complained of having a "worm" in his throat. Sure enough, when the enlarged tonsils came out, a leech came into view. This Harold also removed, much to the patient's relief.

Reflecting on his frequent visits to Al-Hasa in 1944, Harold wrote:

"First, let me mention the other two trips to Hassa this year. Mr. Van Peursem and I went there in March and stayed nearly six weeks. I was then called for a short visit of a few days in August. Both these trips were made in answer to calls from Saud bin Jelowie, Amir of Hassa. The reception from the Amir and his family was most cordial. The people seemed delighted and showed their appreciation by literally swarming to us for treatment.

"This third and last tour was like the other two in that it was a special call from the Amir. We left Bahrain Oct. 11 and returned Nov. 19. We were busy throughout but not as rushed as on the previous tours. The reasons for this were-1. It was right in the midst of the date picking season, 2. It was the time of the Haj and although only a few went many families were very busy and preoccupied. This gave me a little more time to visit and to size up the situation in Hassa as to the possibilities of permanence.

"On both of the long trips this year we were guests of the Amir living in his house and feasting from his bounty. He is a good host and provides well for his guests. Each time we were given a native house and with the aid of cheesecloth and mats soon had a hospital in shape. The Amir expects us to charge the patients

and gives us a free hand in the running of the show. The demands of the royal family are great and sometimes exacting but when we remember that we are his guests we can expect just that.

"Before I left the Amir talked very friendly about my staying and told me that I could stay on for two or three months or as long as I desired."

"The people of Hassa want us."
["Dear Colleagues" letter from Harold Storm dated "Bahrain, Nov. 28, 1944"]

Meanwhile, the World War ended and the hospitals were once again able to procure supplies on a regular basis. While the Bahrain hospitals had experienced more activity than ever before in their history, all in Bahrain had shared in the hardships of the war years following The Great Depression. The emerging petroleum industry and the advent of peace portended a better future. In an article published in the autumn of 1946, Drs. Paul Harrison and Harold Storm reported:

"Two years ago we reported a Christmas gift of Rs. 16,000 from the employees of the Bahrain Petroleum Company, and the B. M. C. Construction Company. This very gracious gift was used for re-equipping our surgical unit. New sterilizers, new tables and a new operating room lamp arrived during the year and now we are proud to show our visitors an operating theater equipped with the latest and best. This evidence of the appreciation of our work among the Arabs on the part of the oil men warmed our hearts."

"Last Christmas we were again surprised by an equally generous gift from the oil

men on the mainland. We intend to use it to re-equip the entire hospital with beds and bedding. This gift from fellow Americans shows heart-warming interest in our work for Arabia and the Arabs."

"Patients from abroad increase in number...."

"Dr. Storm took one long tour of two months into Hassa. Barring the heat, it was a perfect trip. The amount of work done was tremendous and the reception on the part of the government and people most cordial. Hassa is an ideal place for our next forward step. The people want us and are ready for us." ["Our Hospital Takes Stock", *The Church Herald,* October 4, 1946, p. 14]

The medical work remained itinerant despite the wishes of the missionaries. But the stays lengthened. In 1947, Dr. & Mrs. Storm spent eight months in Hofuf, Riyadh and Taif. There was never a lack of work. Rev. Gerrit Van Peursem described the activities of his medical colleagues:

"It is a wonder how the Mission doctor can accomplish so much in a single day and how he can keep up the routine month after month. On tour we get up at dawn and beat the sun.
The Arab has no use for a late sleeper, for 'prayer is better than sleep.' After early breakfast there is a short devotional period with the staff. By that time the patients in the wards demand the attention of doctor and dresser. Often there are more than one hundred inpatients in the wards.
When these patients are cared for, the doctor elbows his way through a crowd of men who almost break his office door to be treated first. Many have never seen an American doctor before, and it's 'first come, first served.' When all these hundreds

are properly diagnosed and treated, it is high noon and time for lunch. Meanwhile, Abd Al Nebi has been busy in the operating room, sterilizing bandages and instruments for the afternoon rush of surgical patients. The doctor may steal his forty winks if he is clever, but by two p.m. he is at it again, performing operations of every conceivable sort--hernia, tumor, amputation, cataract, circumcision, cancer, blood transfusions, etc. Arabia has every disease under the sun, and our doctors are called upon to cure all of them.

King Abdulaziz Al-Saud and Dr. Harold Storm walking together in the 1940's [RCA]

"Supper time arrives one hour after sunset. The whole staff and the missionaries prepare for this by a thorough cleaning and a complete change of clothing. In this way preparation is made for the social evening ahead. At eight p.m. the doctor and the missionary are out calling on friends, eating dates, drinking coffee and tea. These social contacts are valuable and very interesting indeed. Often they recite poetry (the Psalms), and the conversation drifts from politics, language and race to science and religion. In all of it the missionary learns about as much as the Arab. This goes on every evening until as late as eleven p.m. By that time the doctor is willing to admit that he has had a busy, full day.

"Here is what Dr. Storm says in his letter from Taif, dated August 18, 1947. 'I did statistics tonight. In Taif I have done in a little over a month the following:

> *411 operations*
>
> *334 outcalls*
>
> *5422 treatments.'*

"The Storms remained most of their eight months while in the king's country in the three key cities of Hofuf, Riadh and Taif."

"In these three cities men, women and children went to Dr. Storm by the thousands. Rich and poor, men and women, all were treated alike. No man was so poor that he could not get treatment. How many times I have heard Arabs say, 'To the doctor all men are alike.' He does not send bills to the king, but Ibn Saud, being a real king, has never been unmindful of the needs of the Mission. He has a liberal heart. The doctor has never been on a dollar basis; money is secondary with him. His joy and consolation springs from the words of the Apostle Paul in I Cor[inthians] 15:58, 'Therefore, my beloved brethren, be steadfast, immovable, always abounding in the work of the Lord, knowing that in the Lord your labor is not in vain.'" ["The Storms on Trek", *Neglected Arabia*, Number 211, October-December 1947, pp. 9-11]

Such was the attitude of the doctors from Bahrain, and they continued to make the most of every opportunity offered to them to serve the people of the Kingdom of Saudi Arabia. This service often went beyond direct medical care to opening the eyes of the people to the larger world. Dr. Storm's wife Pat was a nurse and accompanied her husband on most of his tours. On a few occasions when all the male personnel on the medical team were otherwise occupied or sick, Pat and the women nurses had the temerity to run the men's clinic. They would only admit a few men at a time to the dispensary. As she reviewed some written instructions regarding medicine with one male patient, he declared it *"haram"* (forbidden) for a woman to read. However, another patient noted that if Pat couldn't read, she would not be able to give out the correct medicines. Even more educated Saudi Arabs of that time period were amazed to discover that Mrs. Storm had a Doctor of Philosophy degree.

As late as 1950, there was still no effective medical service for the general population in Riyadh. A hospital existed with a complement of eleven physicians, but they were not busy. On one trip, Dr. Storm was well occupied in Al-Hasa when summoned to Riyadh by the King. The pace at which things moved once the team arrived in Riyadh frustrated Dr. Storm. It took two weeks to sort out living arrangements. In time, the team was allotted half of the existing hospital space as well as another building where they located their dispensary and operating room.
Mrs. Storm later recounted her experiences of the opening day:

"I shall never forget that first morning when I arrived. The buildings were surrounded by a howling, fighting mob of four hundred people. Harold had sent for a soldier and he was vainly trying to keep the people from trampling each other and breaking in the doors. As the policeman made a way for me through the crowd, women caught me by the abba and tried to show me their afflictions, or held up pitiful, emaciated and half-blind children. From then on, getting through that crowd was the most disagreeable part of my day's work. The soldier sent for reinforcements and from that time until we left, it took six soldiers to keep law

and order." ["Touring Troubles", *Arabia Calling*, Number 218, October 1949-June 1950, pp. 10-11]

While a large volume of work was done, more satisfaction was derived from surgical work that necessarily allowed a longer and closer relationship with the patient and family. Dr. Storm told the story of a night in Riyadh when his sleep was disturbed by a knock on the door:

Dr. Harold Storm and Pat Storm at home in the 1940's [ANS]

"I hastily dressed and went with them through the city gate nearby into the heart of the city and on out through the opposite gate. The city was dead quiet and the stillness of the night was only interrupted by the city guards shouting to one another, 'Saa' thalatha wa kull shay zain'-- three o'clock and all is well. We struggled on in the darkness stumbling over tent pegs and brushing aside half-starved, growling pariah dogs. The only lights were the dying embers of the coffee hearths and an occasional smoking wick in a dish of oil.

"Suddenly we stopped outside one of the tents. There was a command for the

women to get out of the way and an announcement that the doctor had arrived. Children scrambled out of the way from fear. A total stranger had arrived. The place was bare, with no covering on the floor but sand. Mats were lying about on which the family had been asleep.

"Standing just outside the door of the tent was a woman who at once seemed familiar. I had seen her that day and I almost gave an audible laugh as I recognized my patient of that morning. She had come to the women's clinic and on entering my office had stood before my desk silent and unmoved.

"'What is the matter? What is ailing you?', I had asked her.

"'That is what God put you here for, to tell me,' she had replied with all the self-sufficiency and pride of a Bedouin.
"She evidently remembered the incident, for a smile passed over her otherwise impassive face.

"Beside her, lying on the sand, was an old man evidently in great agony.

" 'Abooi, my father,' she said, with tears in her eyes. A glance revealed a very sick man in condition of shock. He was writhing in pain and vomiting profusely. Closer examination revealed a marked swelling on the left inguinal region. The diagnosis was not difficult -- strangulated hernia. An operation was imperative."

"I talked; I persuaded; women consulted with each other; men agreed; women disagreed, and then we started all over again. Meanwhile, attracted by the noise, the little kids came into the tent to see what was going on. Soon their mother came looking for them and bleating her disapproval. The children, having discovered that the doctor was being accepted by the family, came out of their hiding and added to the general confusion by chasing the goats out of the tent.

"Much to my surprise the patient of the morning spoke up. 'They will take good care of him. There are many people being operated upon by this doctor at Beit Zeke,' (house of Zeke) -- our temporary hospital.

"Her counsel prevailed. They carried the old man back through the city to Beit Zeke. We spent the rest of the night operating. Uneventful recovery returned the old man to his tent."

"Before returning to our base I paid a visit to this tent. There was nothing strange about my coming this time. Children were not afraid. There was no commotion as before. The old man greeted me as he would have greeted a son." ["El-Khokha --The Little Door", *Arabia Calling*, Number 225, October-December 1951, pp. 10-11]

Nurse Cornelia Dalenberg en route to Al-Hasa in the 1940's
[ANS]

Chapter 12

*There is an end
to all things*

r. Gerald Nykerk had been with the Arabian Mission since 1941. In February of 1950, he received his first invitation to Al-Hasa, about which he wrote:

"...it pleased us a great deal to find King Ibn Saoud's representatives in Bahrain coming to us with a formal request from the Emir Bin Jaluie of Hassa, asking that our doctor come to Hassa at once to perform an operation on the daughter of the Emir. They were anxious for us to come at once. We immediately packed up boxes and boxes of medicines and supplies and were ready in two days' time. The group consisted of the Nykerk family, including the children, Miss Nellie

Dr. Gerald Nykerk
about 1950
[ANS]

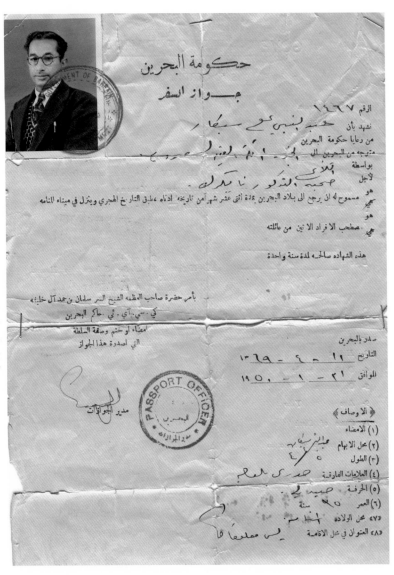

Abdulnabi Sabkar's Passport document permitting him to accompany Dr. Nykerk to Saudi Arabia [ANS]

Hekhuis, R.N., our nurse, and the Rev. Luidens, our pastor...and four hospital helpers.

"A day after our arrival we made arrangements for the operation on the Emir's daughter, which was performed in a large and picturesque mejlis in the palace itself. The following day we set up a clinic in an Arab home, cleaned out the old unused building formerly used as hospital and operating room on previous tours, and began to work.

"I have never seen so many people in such a small area who needed so much medical attention. Our clinics were so large that we could not possibly see the crowds that gathered daily. Eye disease and tuberculosis were predominant and we treated 5,495 patients and performed 242 operations in our stay of less than two months, and yet we only touched the surface of what needs to be done.

"The operation on the Emir's daughter proved to be successful. God blessed our work among the people, and they begged us not to leave them. Oh, that the way might be opened to enter Hafoof to begin a mission hospital there." ["Following the Great Physician", *The Church Herald*, April 6, 1951; pp. 4, 20]

*The Nykerk family with
Bahraini friends
about 1950 [ANS]*

These final words reflect what had always been the desire of the missionaries -- to establish a permanent presence in the Kingdom of Saudi Arabia. But shortly after writing the account of his trip to Hofuf, Dr. Nykerk contracted tuberculosis and had to take a long leave of absence in the United States. Because of this, the Bahrain hospitals had to withdraw from another field of activity -- Doha, Qatar. With such limited personnel resources, it became difficult to support tours into the Kingdom of Saudi Arabia. In response to this situation, Dr. Paul Harrison returned from his retirement and served at the Mason Memorial Hospital in Bahrain from 1952 until 1954 thus enabling Dr. Storm to continue making tours on the mainland.

The tours in the first half of the 1950's were all to Hofuf. The medical teams never lacked for work to do among the people of Al-Hasa, and many others came from distant parts of the Kingdom because of the reputation the mission medical teams had earned. But there were palpable

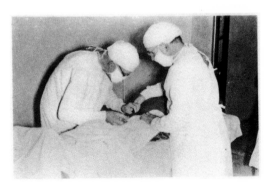

Dr. Paul Harrison & Dr. Harold Storm at work in the operating room at Mason Memorial Hospital
[RCA]

Dr. Paul & Ann Harrison in the 1950's
[ANS]

changes taking place at many levels within Saudi Arabia. Some of these were noted in the reports submitted by the doctors to their constituents in the United States. Dr. Storm wrote:

"The trip to Hassa in 1951 was unique in several ways. It was the first tour to the mainland made without a special invitation to treat some specific individual. It was the first time that we were permitted to live freely, doing our own housekeeping, and living as ordinary citizens of the place and not as guests. The greatest change was the large number of women who came out to the clinics. Hitherto the women of Hassa had not come out in large numbers, but this time, three days a week, we had from 250 to 300 women every morning. We also felt that definite progress was made in the attitude of the wealthy merchant class toward the tour. They seemed more interested than ever before, were even ashamed of the wretched house given to us for a hospital, and told me they had presented a petition to the Amir asking that we stay permanently in Hassa. The outcome of this petition was that we were told to leave our things and return after the summer."

"This interest on the part of the merchant class and the ready acquiescence of the Amir to their request seems to be an indication that Hassa is just about ready for the mission to consider taking up the work there. It seems important for us to make the best of this opportunity because life has changed so completely in the Nejd that the need on the part of the ruling class for mission doctors is not nearly so acute as it was even ten years ago, and will be even less in the years to come. If the mission doctors are not permitted to enter at this opportunity, it may be that the opportunity will not recur...." ["Mason Memorial Hospital in Bahrain", *The Church Herald*, February 8, 1952; p. 16]

There were other issues. The mission personnel had always coupled a concern for the souls of humans with the care of their physical bodies. Restrictions were placed upon the spiritual activities of the missionaries. Furthermore, the hospitals of the American Mission were no longer the dominant players in the Gulf countries. In 1953, Dr. Harrison wrote:

"The Persian Gulf Medical Society met in Saudi Arabia this year. We were guests of Aramco, the great oil company which works in that country. The mission hospitals of Muscat, Kuwait and Bahrain are members of the society, but we form a small minority. Oil company hospitals in Kuwait, and Qatar, and Bahrain, together with government hospitals in those same communities, are large and well-equipped, very impressive affairs." ["New Era in Medical Missions", *The Church Herald*, February 19, 1954; p. 17]

The house in Hofuf used as a hospital during the final tours to Al-Hasa in the 1950's. [AMH]

Dr. Storm was even more direct in his comments as recorded in the "Annual Report of the Mason Memorial Hospital, Bahrain, Arabia, for the year 1954."

"There is another obstacle which can be a blessing as well as a hardship. The rich and ruling classes do not need us as in former years. Improvement in travel,

company medical set-ups, can and will care for many. This leaves us a better opportunity to care for the common people.

On the other hand the fact that the rich and ruling classes do not need us makes our permanent permission to remain in the country more difficult."

The desired permission never came. In fact, greater obstacles were placed before the mission medical teams. They were asked for higher and higher rents for the buildings they used. Import duties and various other taxes were imposed. The medical tours had always created financial strains on the mission, and now the situation became well nigh impossible. After 1955, there were no further invitations for the teams to return. In 1956, a brief trip was made to Hofuf to recoup equipment and supplies that had been left, and this aspect of the American Mission's activity quietly ended.

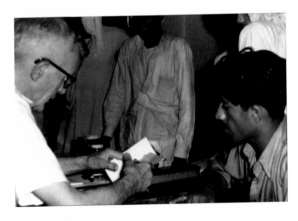

Dr. Paul Harrison caring for a patient
in the clinic in the 1950's
[AMH]

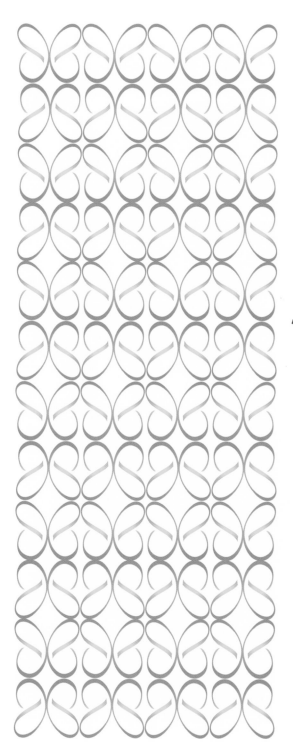

PostScript

Postscript

American Mission Hospital Today

In 1962, the *Amir* of Bahrain, *Shaikh* Isa bin Sulman Al-Khalifa, cut a ribbon to open the new buildings of American Mission Hospital. The old Mason Memorial Hospital had been demolished and the Marion Wells Thoms Memorial Hospital was integrated into the new complex, which was now operated as a single entity.

Shaikh Isa Bin Sulman Al-Khalifa, the Patron of the newly formed
American Mission Hospital Society with the AMH Board, 1988
[AMH]

In March of 1988, American Mission Hospital (AMH) was reorganized by Ministerial Decree as the American Mission Hospital Society - Bahrain. A new constitution was designed by the Ministry of Labour & Social Affairs in order to retain the traditional character of the hospital, while giving it a structure to support future growth and development. The hospital remains a not-for-profit organization without shareholders. Any financial surpluses earned by the hospital are used to expand and improve its services or to provide charitable assistance to deserving individuals. A governing board of twelve directors and four observers are drawn from the community and serve without remuneration.

Construction underway of the AMH 2000 Building, winter 2000 [AMH]

The new AMH buildings shortly after completion in the summer of 2000 [AMH]

The old and the new AMH buildings shortly after completion in the summer of 2000 [AMH]

Since its inception in 1988, the American Mission Hospital Society - Bahrain, has moved from strength to strength. At the beginning, a staff of nine physicians and surgeons served approximately 100-150 patients each day. Today, a staff of forty doctors and six dentists serve 400-500 patients each day. Services are available to the public 24-hours a day, seven days of the week. Every attempt is made to keep prices and costs as low as possible. Constant improvements are being made in the range of diagnostic and treatment capabilities offered. Quality is emphasized throughout. The result is a continuing high level of trust between the hospital and the people it serves.

For some years, the need for new buildings for AMH has been apparent. The structures in use in 1988 were antiquated and too small to accommodate significant growth. Adjacent land was purchased in 1995. A plan for rebuilding AMH was then put before the late *Amir*, *Shaikh* Isa bin Sulman Al-Khalifa, who encouraged the hospital's Board of Directors to proceed.

Two physicians, a practical nurse and a patient in the clinic at American Mission Hospital in 2001
[AMH]

Mason Memorial Hospital, Bahrain [RCA]

Marion Wells Thoms Memorial Hospital, Bahrain [RCA]

The American Mission Hospital - 100 years of service in Bahrain.
[AMH]

In addition, the *Amir* made a very generous donation toward the rebuilding project. An aggressive program of fund-raising was begun jointly with the American Association of Bahrain (AAB). Over five years, the AAB-AMH Island Classic charity golf tournament and associated events succeeded in raising a total of BD1,300,000 ($3,456,000). Using some additional funds from AMH reserves, the hospital was able to complete the first phase of its rebuilding program providing 6125 square meters of new space at a cost of BD1,520,000 ($4,053,000).

Phase 2 of the AMH rebuilding program will provide new clinics, inpatient units, surgical, diagnostic and treatment facilities. A 9000 square meter building is envisioned. Given the high costs of new equipment for units such as Diagnostic Imaging and the Operating Rooms, it is estimated that this project will cost BD4,000,000 ($10,666,000).

The need for high quality, affordable, private medical and dental care in the Arabian Gulf region is apparent. Governments seek ways to limit their financial exposure while continuing to support the provision of medical and dental services for their people. Health insurers everywhere are looking for providers who can offer high quality services without losing sight of the need for cost controls. AMH, as a not-for-profit institution, fulfills these criteria and can give leadership to the development of private sector medical and dental services in a growing and changing environment, as it has done for the past one hundred years.

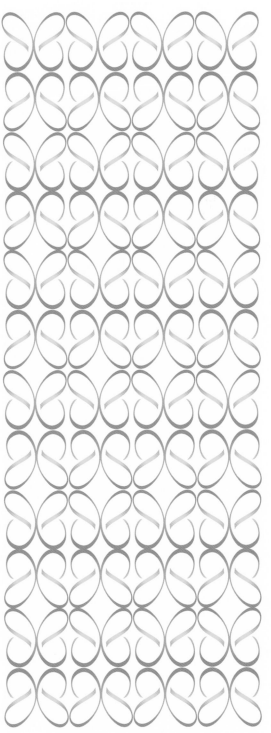

Chronology

Chronology of Work Accomplished in the Kingdom of Saudi Arabia 1913 - 1955

Year, Personalities and Places Visited

1913   Dr. Paul Harrison held clinics in Qatif

1914   The *Sultan* of the Nejd, *Shaikh* Abdulaziz Al Saud, gave an audience to Dr. Stanley Mylrea in his camp outside Kuwait City during the month of May. Dr. Mylrea removed a tumor from the arm of *Shaikh* Hafiz Al-Wahba, later the Ambassador of the Kingdom of Saudi Arabia to the United Kingdom. He also treated many other sick men in *Shaikh* Abdulaziz's camp.

Dr. Paul Harrison and Mrs. Josephine Van Peursem held clinics and performed surgery in Qatif for a month and a half during the early summer. The numbers attended were "quite overwhelming".

1915   Dr. Paul Harrison held clinics in Qatif for "several" weeks.

1916   Dr. Hall Van Vlack was called to Riyadh to treat *Shaikh* Abdulaziz Al Saud but was turned back at Hofuf because the *Sultan* had recovered.

Shaikh Jabr of Kuwait brought his guests, *Shaikh* Abdulaziz Al Saud and *Shaikh* Khazad of Muhammerah, to the home of Dr. Stanley Mylrea during a visit the *sheyukh* made to Kuwait in November.

1917   Dr. Paul Harrison was called to Darin for six weeks during June and July to treat an obstetrical case. Thereafter, he treated many pearl divers.

Immediately upon his return to Bahrain, the *Sultan* of the Nejd, *Shaikh* Abdulaziz Al Saud, called Dr. Harrison to Riyadh for a medical trip that lasted one month.

1918   Dr. Paul Harrison made a two-day visit to *Shaikh* Jassim of Dhahran to arrange for future medical work.

1918-1919 Dr. Paul Harrison was called urgently to Riyadh by the *Sultan* of the Nejd, *Shaikh* Abdulaziz Al Saud, in order to help combat the worldwide Influenza epidemic that was taking so many lives in the Saudi capital. Dr. Harrison arrived after the death of the king's eldest son, Turki, but he was able to assist many who were convalescing and helped organize better distribution of food and supplies in the city. In the course of his return to Bahrain, he stopped for two weeks in Hofuf where he saw many patients and performed fifty surgeries.

1919   Dr. Paul Harrison held clinics in Qatif.

1920   Dr. Paul Harrison held clinics in Al-Hasa for two months.

            Dr. Louis Dame left on November 17 for a six-week medical
            visit to Riyadh at the request of the *Sultan* of the Nejd, *Shaikh*
            Abdulaziz Al Saud.

1922   Dr. Louis Dame responded to urgent calls to care for patients
            in Al-Hasa and Qatif.

1923   Dr. Louis Dame made two medical trips, one to Al-Hasa for
            three weeks and another to Qatif for one week.

            Dr. Dame left Bahrain November 6, 1923, and returned
            March 15, 1924. This began as a planned tour. However, while
            en route to Riyadh, Dr. Dame was called urgently to attend
            Shaikh Abdulaziz Al Saud, who was suffering from a severe
            infection in his face. Dr. Dame was able to cure his royal patient,
            and the *Sultan* celebrated with a great reception.

            Dr. Dame toured further inland from Riyadh to Shaqra, Oneiza
            and Buraidah. During the four months and seven days spent
            in the Sultanate of the Nejd and its dependencies, a total of
            6,552 patients were treated, 128 major and 214 minor operations
            were performed, 81 injections were given, and many house calls
            were made. Forty-one days were spent travelling on the backs
            of camels and donkeys.

1924   Dr. Louis Dame made a medical tour into Eastern Arabia.

1925   Dr. Louis Dame made a medical tour into Eastern Arabia.

1926   Dr. Harrison visited Qatif in February to arrange for a medical
            visit after *Ramadhan*. Lady nurses later worked in Qatif.

1927   A medical tour was made to Dammam and Qatif.

1929   Dr. Louis Dame was invited to Al-Hasa on four separate
            occasions. He treated Prince Saud, the eldest son of King
            Abdulaziz Al Saud, as well as Ibn Jalawi, the Governor of the
            Eastern Province.

1930   Dr. Louis Dame spent three and one half months working in
            Al-Hasa.

1931   Dr. Louis Dame traveled via Qatif to Jubail to treat the local
            Amir in February.

            In April,   Dr. Dame was called to Al-Hasa to treat two officials.
            In June, Dr. Dame spent another three weeks doing medical
            work in Al-Hasa.

1932   Dr. Louis Dame made a seventy-four day medical tour to the
                  Hejaz and Taif and treated King Abdulaziz, members of the

King's family, the *Amir* of Jeddah, and the Keeper of the Keys of the *Ka'aba* (the holiest shrine of Islam in Mecca).

1933   Dr. Louis Dame and several others left Bahrain on July 26 and arrived in Riyadh on August 2. They returned to Bahrain on October 25. During this time they gave 3,267 treatments, performed 130 operations and made 221 house calls.

Additional trips were made to Hofuf, Wadi Hanifah, and Dhahran.

1934   Dr. Louis Dame made another medical trip to Riyadh.

1935   Dr. Louis Dame left Bahrain on February 18 for the Nejd. In Riyadh, Dr. Dame and his helpers saw an average of 400 patients each day.
After spending several weeks in Riyadh, Dr. Dame left for Hail on April 15. Dr. Dame and company returned to Bahrain during August.

Dr. Harold Storm joined Dr. Dame in Riyadh during mid-June. Dr. Storm and his company spent eight months touring the Arabian Peninsula. This included a six-week stay in Taif where they gave 4475 treatments, 1841 injections, performed 87 operations and made 274 house calls.
Dr. Wells Thoms did medical work in Al-Hasa for two and one half weeks.

1936   Staff members of the Bahrain hospitals made "several tours" in the Kingdom of Saudi Arabia.

Dr. Wells Thoms worked in Al-Hasa during November and December.

1937   Dr. Wells Thoms left Bahrain on January 6, for Riyadh. He stayed there for forty days, treated "thousands" of patients and performed more than 300 operations.

Crown Prince Saud Ibn Abdulaziz and Prince Mohammed Ibn Abdudaziz visited the Amir of Bahrain, *Shaikh* Hamad bin Isa Al-Khalifa, and the American Mission's hospitals in Bahrain during the month of December.

1938   Dr. Louis Dame and Dr. Esther Barny worked in Riyadh during the autumn.

1939   Dr. Esther Barny worked in Riyadh.

Nurse Cornelia Dalenberg worked for four months in Al-Hasa.

Dr. Louis Dame worked in Riyadh from August to November. He would have left sooner, but on October 7, Crown Prince Saud broke his arm in an equestrian accident. Dr. Dame remained in Riyadh and successfully treated the Prince's fracture. During this visit, 140 operations were performed.

1940   Dr. Esther Barny spent four months working in Riyadh.

Nurse Cornelia Dalenberg made an "extensive" medical tour of Al-Hasa during November and December.

1941   Dr. and Mrs. Paul Harrison went to Al-Hasa in mid-December and returned at the end of January 1942. During this time, they spent 2 weeks in Riyadh at the request of King Abdulaziz Al Saud.

1942   Frequent tours were made to Riyadh and the Nejd.

Dr. Paul Harrison worked in Al-Hasa and Riyadh from January to March.

Dr. Paul Harrison and Dr. Esther Barny worked in Riyadh from mid-August until October 1 at the request of King Abdulaziz Al Saud.

1943   Dr. Harold Storm spent six weeks in Riyadh and Qatif from January 27 until March 10. Dr. Esther Barny joined the group in Riyadh. A total of 4000 treatments were conducted, and Dr. Storm performed 316 eye operations.

1944   Dr. Esther Barny Ames spent the month of February in Riyadh at the request of King Abdulaziz Al Saud.

Dr. Harold Storm spent six weeks during March and April in Al-Hasa during which time he treated 3000 patients, performed 392 operations and made 205 house calls.

Dr. Storm made another visit to Qatif from August 10 to 12.

Dr. Ames spent much of September and October in Riyadh.

Dr. Storm returned to work in Al-Hasa from October 11 to November 19.

1945   Dr. Harold Storm worked in Al-Hasa from June 4 until August 9.

1947   Dr. Harold Storm and company left for Al-Hasa on January 10. They ended up remaining in the Kingdom of Saudi Arabia for a total of eight months and eight days including one and one half months in Al-Hasa, four months in Riyadh and two and one half months in Taif. During this time, 29,229 treatments were given, 1600 operations were performed, and 2728 house calls were made. They returned to Bahrain on September 11.

1948   "Several trips" were made to Riyadh and Hofuf at the request of King Abdulaziz Al Saud.

1950   Dr. Gerald Nykerk visited Al-Hasa during February to perform surgery on the daughter of the *Amir* Saud Ibn Jalawi. This visit extended over seven weeks until supplies were exhausted. A total of 5495 patients were treated and 242 operations were done.

1951   Dr. Harold Storm made a medical tour of Al-Hasa from February 1 until June 2. A total of 15,705 patients were treated, 162 major and 936 minor operations were performed and 826 house calls were made.

        Dr. Harold Storm worked in Riyadh during November.

1952-1953 Dr. Storm and company left for Al-Hasa in December and remained for five months. They treated 14,698 patients, performed 285 major and 685 minor operations, and made 718 house calls.

1953-1954 Dr. Harold Storm and company worked in Al-Hasa from October 12 until April 29. A total of 9,382 patients were treated and 255 surgical operations were performed.

1954-1955 Dr. Harold Storm and Dr. Bernard Voss worked in Al-Hasa from late December to mid-April. Dr. Donald Bosch briefly joined them during January. Together they treated 6,266 patients, performed 103 major operations and 201 minor operations.

Key Personalities in this Book

Identification of Key Personalities and Organizations in This Book

Kings, Governors and Citizens of Saudi Arabia

Abdulaziz Ibn Abdulrahman Al Saud, Abd'al Aziz Al Saud, Abdul Aziz Ibn Saud, Ibn Saud, Ibn Sa'ud, Ibn Saoud: circa1876-1953; founder and first ruler of the modern Kingdom of Saudi Arabia. He took control of Riyadh, the capital city of the Nejd, by a daring dawn raid in 1902. He conquered the Turkish garrison in Hofuf with another surprise attack in May, 1913 and completed his conquests by taking over the Hejaz and entering Mecca as a pilgrim in December, 1924. Beginning as a *shaikh* from a powerful family, he became the *Sultan* of the Nejd and its Dependencies until, in 1927, he was declared King of Hejaz and Nejd and its Dependencies. His country was officially named the Kingdom of Saudi Arabia in 1932. He succeeded in organizing a modern nation and positioned it to take full advantage of the tremendous mineral wealth that lay buried beneath its surface.

Saud Ibn Abudulaziz Al Saud: 1902-1969; made Crown Prince in 1933, then became the second ruler of the Kingdom of Saudi Arabia upon the death of his father in 1953. He reigned until ill health led to his replacement by his brother Faisal in 1964.

Faisal Ibn Abdulaziz Al Saud: reigned as King from 1964 until his assassination in 1975.

Khalid Ibn Abdulaziz Al Saud: reigned as King from 1975 until his death in 1982.

Fahd Ibn Abdulaziz Al Saud: has reigned as King from 1982 until the present time.

Abdulla Ibn Jalawi, Abd'allah Ibn Jaloui, Ibn Jelowie, Ibn Jaluie: a cousin of King Abudulaziz Al Saud, he was one of the King's faithful warriors. He is reputed to have breached the gate of Riyadh in the attack of 1902. He was made Governor of the Eastern Province after it was conquered in 1913.

Saud Ibn Abdulla Ibn Jalawi: second governor of the Eastern Province

Abdulrahman Al-Gosaibi: a leading member of a large merchant family in the Eastern Province and also Bahrain, who acted as agents for King Abdulaziz in Bahrain. In 1926, this family donated land for the construction of the Marion Wells Thoms Memorial Hospital.

Rulers of Bahrain

Isa bin Ali Al-Khalifa: *Amir* 1869-1932.

Hamad bin Isa Al-Khalifa: *Amir* 1932-1942.

Salman bin Hamad Al-Khalifa: *Amir* 1942-1961.

Isa bin Salman Al-Khalifa: *Amir* 1961-1999.

Hamad bin Isa Al-Khalifa: *Amir* 1999-2002, King 2002-

The American Mission

Reformed Church in America: originally an extension of the Dutch Reformed Church, its active ministry began in the Dutch colonies of the New World in 1628. Following the American Revolution, the church was organized as an independent denomination in the United States. From the early years of the 19th century, the Reformed Church was active in foreign mission enterprises.

Arabian Mission: independently established in 1889 to support a pioneer missionary effort in the Arabian Peninsula, the Arabian Mission was adopted by the Reformed Church in 1894. Its first field station was Basrah, Iraq, followed by Bahrain, Oman, Amarah in Iraq, and finally Kuwait.

The mission as a distinct entity was dissolved in 1973. Daughter institutions continue in Bahrain, Oman and Kuwait.

American Mission: the name given to the Arabian Mission stations in the Gulf States. It became incorporated into an official name only in Bahrain when the hospitals were combined under the name "American Mission Hospital" in 1962.

Samuel Zwemer: a founder and one of the two pioneer missionaries who established the Arabian Mission in the Gulf region. He arrived in the Gulf in early 1892 and joined his colleague James Cantine in Basrah, Iraq, where they established their first station. Zwemer developed an outstation in Bahrain in 1893 and then settled there in 1896. He made several exploratory trips into eastern Arabia in the 1890's. He actively recruited doctors for the Arabian Mission and had much to do with the construction of the first hospital in the Arabian Gulf, the Mason Memorial Hospital in Bahrain.

Sharon Thoms, MD: appointed in 1898, studied Arabic in Basrah 1898-1900, served in Bahrain from 1900 until 1909 when he transferred to Oman. He died as the result of an accident sustained while serving in Oman in 1913. Sharon Thoms was the physician who guided the process of constructing and fitting out the Mason Memorial Hospital in Bahrain. He was the father of Wells Thoms.

Marion Wells Thoms, MD: wife of Sharon Thoms, also appointed in 1898, studied Arabic in Basrah 1898-1900, and served in Bahrain from 1900 until her untimely death from typhoid fever in 1905. She was the mother of Wells Thoms.

C. Stanley G. Mylrea, MD: appointed 1906, studied Arabic and served in Bahrain 1907-1912, then following a furlough was reassigned to Kuwait in 1914 where he served until retiring in 1941. He returned to Bahrain in 1944 and served until he retired again in 1947. Dr. Mylrea was the first doctor of the mission to have contact with King Abdulaziz Al Saud.

Paul Harrison, MD: appointed 1909, arrived in Basrah, Iraq, in 1910 where he studied Arabic until transferred to the new outstation in Kuwait in 1911. In 1913, he transferred to Bahrain and served there until 1922. He returned to Kuwait in 1924, transferred to Bahrain again in 1925, served in Oman 1928-1938, and yet again in Bahrain from 1941 until he departed on furlough in 1948 and retired in 1949. Like Mylrea before him, he returned from retirement to serve in Bahrain one more time 1952-1954. Dr. Harrison led the mission's first medical tours in Saudi Arabia, initially to the Eastern Province, then to Riyadh.

Gerrit Van Peursem: appointed and arrived in Bahrain in 1910. Served in Oman 1918-1930, Bahrain 1933-1946, and retired in 1947. Rev. Van Peursem frequently accompanied his wife Josephine, a nurse, and the doctors who toured Saudi Arabia. He was personally acquainted with King Abudulaziz Al Saud and discussed comparative religion with him on several occasions.

Josephine Van Peursem: appointed as a single nurse in 1910, she arrived in Bahrain that same year. She married Rev. Gerrit Van Peursem in 1913.

Thereafter, her career paralleled that of her husband. As a nurse often serving without the support of a female physician, she was called upon to administer a broad range of services for female patients. She accompanied the mission physicians on tours of Saudi Arabia beginning in 1914 and extending into the 1940's. With her husband, she retired in 1947.

Louis Dame, MD: appointed 1919, arrived in Bahrain the same year to begin language study and remained to serve in Bahrain until 1936 when Dr. Dame transferred to California Arabian Standard Oil Company (CASOC) in Dhahran, Saudi Arabia. Dr. Dame provided extensive amounts of medical service to King Abdulaziz Al Saud, his family and his subjects, and received international recognition for his accounts of his travels in Saudi Arabia.

Elizabeth Dame: wife of Dr. Louis Dame, appointed in 1919 and served in Bahrain until 1936. She was an educator, and ran a school for girls in Bahrain. In the 1930's, she frequently accompanied her husband on his trips to the interior of Saudi Arabia and left some excellent accounts of these tours.

Cornelia Dalenberg: a nurse, appointed in 1921 and arrived in Bahrain to study Arabic 1921-1923. She served in Bahrain 1923-1929; Basrah, Iraq in 1930; Amarah, Iraq 1931-1944 with a brief period in Bahrain in 1940; Bahrain 1945-1955; Oman 1956; Kuwait 1958; and finally Bahrain 1959-1961. She made several tours into Saudi Arabia and Qatar, many of these independently.

Esther Barny Ames, M.D: born in 1902 in Basrah, Iraq, to missionaries Fred and Margaret Barny. Appointed in 1927 and proceeded to Baghdad for Arabic studies. She served in Kuwait 1929-1932 and Bahrain 1937-1945. She married John Ames, an employee of Standard Oil, in 1943. As a mission physician, she made several tours in Saudi Arabia. She and her husband evidently spent some years living in Dhahran, Saudi Arabia, because Dr. Harold Storm called upon her to assist him during some of his later tours in Al-Hasa.

Harold Storm, MD: appointed 1926, proceeded to Kuwait and then Bahrain for language study 1927-1929. Served at Amarah, Iraq, 1929-1930; Oman 1931-1932 where his first wife died after childbirth; Bahrain 1934 until he retired in 1965. He toured extensively during his career, especially in Saudi Arabia and Qatar, and left detailed accounts of his experiences.

Ida Patterson Storm, Ph.D: formerly a missionary in China, she studied nursing so that she could assist her husband's work. She married Dr. Harold Storm in 1935 and served in Bahrain with him until their retirement in 1965. She accompanied him on several tours in Saudi Arabia and left colorful accounts of her experiences.

Wells Thoms, MD: son of Sharon and Marion Wells Thoms, the original physicians to serve at Mason Memorial Hospital in Bahrain. Wells was appointed in 1933 and came to Bahrain that same year. In 1938 he was assigned to Kuwait; then to Oman in 1939 where he remained until retirement in 1970.

Gerald Nykerk, MD: appointed 1940, arrived in Bahrain in 1941 to begin Arabic studies. This he completed in Kuwait in 1943 and remained there to serve until 1950 when he transferred to Bahrain. In 1951, Dr. Nykerk was diagnosed with tuberculosis and took medical leave in the USA for 2 years. He returned to Amarah, Iraq, in 1954 and remained there until the Iraqi Government expropriated the hospital in 1958. He then served in Bahrain 1959-1961, and Kuwait from 1963 until his untimely death of a heart attack in 1964.

Donald Bosch, MD: appointed in 1950; assigned to Amarah, Iraq, for language study and initial service 1951-1954; participated in a tour to Hofuf while briefly in Bahrain in early 1955; served in Oman from 1955 until his retirement with occasional periods in Kuwait and Bahrain.

Bernard Voss, MD: appointed in 1951, studied Arabic in Kuwait 1952, assigned to Bahrain in 1953. Served in Bahrain until the end of 1956 and then resigned from the mission.

Others of Note

Mubarak Al Sabah, "Mubarak the Great": ruler of Kuwait from 1896-1915. He brought Kuwait under British protection in 1899. He was a close associate of *Shaikh* Abdulaziz Al Saud. In the 1890's, he assisted the future King in his study of foreign affairs. In 1901, *Shaikh* Mubarrak and *Shaikh* Abdulaziz joined forces against the Rashidis of Hail.

Harry St. John Philby, a.k.a. Abdulla Philby: first became acquainted with King Abdulaziz Al Saud as a British military representative in 1917-1918. Moved to Jiddah in 1926 to set up a trading business, but maintained close contact with the King and acted as an advisor to him. He converted to Islam in 1930, was married locally, and remained close to the Al Sauds for the rest of his life.

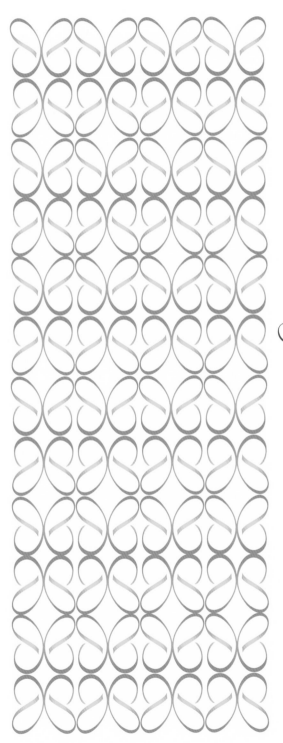

Glossary & Gazetteer

Glossary of Medical, Arabic and Other Unusual Terms or Names

abba, abbaya	:	a lightweight black overcloak worn in public by Arab women of the Gulf region
abscess	:	an infection characterized by a collection of pus
abu	:	father of...
amir, emir	:	a ruler at the level of prince
ARAMCO	:	the Arabian American Oil Company. The original concession to search for oil was given to the Standard Oil Company of California [SOCAL] in 1933. SOCAL formed a new subsidiary in 1934 called California Arabian Standard Oil Company [CASOC] and assigned it the concession. In 1944, CASOC was renamed the Arabian American Oil Company which was shortened to ARAMCO. By the early 1980's, ARAMCO became wholly owned by the Kingdom of Saudi Arabia.

bait, beit	:	house
bedu, bedouin,		
fem. *bedouiya*	:	desert dweller
bin	:	see *ibn*
bint	:	daughter of...
cellulitis	:	a diffuse infection of soft tissue
chloroform	:	an anesthetic agent
comminuted fracture	:	a fracture of bone resulting in multiple fragments.
compound fracture	:	a fracture of bone with penetration of the overlying skin; an open fracture
condyle	:	a projection from the shaft of a bone that supports an articular surface of a joint.
Flit	:	a brand of insecticide that was supplied in a pump-spray apparatus.
haj, hajj	:	the annual pilgrimage to Mecca; the month of the pilgrimage.
hakim, fem. *hakima*	:	a wise person; a doctor.
hernia	:	a defect in the connective tissues of the wall of the abdomen
house officer	:	a physician in a hospital-based, post-graduate training program; a resident.
humerus	:	the bone between the shoulder and the elbow joints.
ibn	:	son of...
influenza	:	a type of contagious bacterial respiratory infection

trichiasis : a turning inward of the eyelids such that the lashes irritate the eye; results from inflammation of the mucus membranes of the eyelid such as occurs with trachoma.

tuberculosis : an infection caused by a type of bacteria that is resistant to treatment; usually infects the lungs via inhalation but may also be swallowed and cause infections of the GI tract and elsewhere.

um : mother of...

wadi, wady : a river bed or small valley, usually dry, running through a desert.

Wahabi : follower of, or pertaining to a conservative interpretation of Islam, named for the 18th century reformer Mohammed Ibn Abdulwahab; predominant in the Kingdom of Saudi Arabia.

Gazetteer of Current and Historical Place Names

Any exercise in which place names are taken from one language and script into another is fraught with difficulty. In compiling this list, I have generally shown the English spellings in official use within the respective countries followed by the variant spellings that are found within quotations in the text. Where a place name in the old accounts begins with a different letter, I have listed it separately and referred the reader to the contemporary spelling. Otherwise, I have just grouped the various spellings together.

A few places referred to within quotations in the text have been identified only on the basis of those descriptions as I have been unable to find corresponding names or locations on contemporary maps. These are noted with an asterisk.*

Finally, there is the matter of the definite article "Al" in Arabic, which properly precedes many of the names listed below. When searching for a place name in an atlas or using a search engine, if results are not obtained with a name as shown below, add Al or Al- before the name. If that does not work, substitute the first letter of the place name for the letter l in the definite article, e.g. Ad Dawadimi or Ar Riyadh.

Abqaiq	:	a village, and later a secondary ARAMCO oil camp in the Eastern Province of Saudi Arabia, located between Uqair and Hofuf.
Abu Jifan	:	an oasis on the Hofuf-Riyadh caravan route, just east of the Dahna Sands.
Afif, Bier Afeef	:	a town 295 kilometers west and slightly south of Riyadh.
Ainain	:	see 'Uyaynah
Al-Hasa, Al-Hassa	:	oasis region inland from the east coast of Saudi Arabia.
Al-Khobar, Al-Khubar	:	a harbor on the east coast of Saudi Arabia near Bahrain.
Anieza	:	see Oneiza
Arabian Gulf	:	the preferred name among the Arab countries that line its shores for the body of water bordered by Iran, Iraq, Kuwait, Saudi Arabia, Qatar, the United Arab Emirates and Oman, and in which the Islands of Bahrain lie.
Ared Hills, Jebel 'Urayd;	:	hills just west of Jebel Tuwayk about 110 kilometers west-northwest of Riyadh.
Ared-Washem Plateau	:	a land formation northwest of Riyadh adjacent to Jebel 'Urayd and immediately west of Jebel Tuwayk.*

'Arier, Arrayrah	:	see Uray'irah
Awained	:	see Uwaynid
Bahrain, Bahrein	:	an emirate (princedom) ruled by an *emir* or *amir*. During the period under consideration in this volume, Bahrain was a protectorate of Great Britain. Independent since 1971, it was declared a Kingdom in 2001.
Basrah, Basra	:	a city in Iraq below the confluence of the Tigris and Euphrates Rivers.
Bier Afeef	:	see Afif
Budaiya	:	a fishing village on the northwest corner of Bahrain Island.
Burrah, Burra	:	a town 90 kilometers west-northwest of Riyadh.
Buraidah, Boreida, Barada	:	a town in central Arabia between Riyadh and Hail.
Dahna Sands	:	a broad swathe of red-orange sand dunes running northwest to southeast in central Saudi Arabia, lying 80 kilometers east of Riyadh.
Dammam	:	a harbor on the east coast of Saudi Arabia near Bahrain.
Darin, Dareen	:	an island-fishing village on the east coast of Saudi Arabia near Qatif.

Dhahran	:	*Jebel* (Mountain) Dhahran was the site of the Dammam dome, the first productive oil field discovered in the Eastern Province of the Kingdom of Saudi Arabia; later the site of the ARAMCO oil camp; located just inland between the ports of Dammam and Al-Khobar.
Diriyah, Dir'iyyah, Deraiyah	:	an old capital of the Nejd, now a ruin, just northwest of Riyadh in Wadi Hanifa.
Dowadimi, Dowadamie	:	a town 235 kilometers west of Riyadh
Eastern Province	:	the eastern part of the Kingdom of Saudi Arabia including the Arabian Gulf coast.
Hail	:	a city in the north-central region of Saudi Arabia.
Hejaz, Hedjaz	:	the western part of the Kingdom of Saudi Arabia including the Red Sea coast.
Hofuf, Hufuf, Hofhuf, Hofhoof, Hafoof	:	the main city of the Al-Hasa Oasis.
Jebel Tuwayk, Jebel Tuwaik	:	a mountain range running north and south immediately west of Riyadh.
Jiddah, Jeddah	:	the port city for Mecca, situated centrally on the Red Sea coast of Saudi Arabia.

Jubayl, Jubail, Jebeel	:	a port 80 kilometers north of Dammam on the east coast of Saudi Arabia.
Jubaylah, Jubaila	:	an oasis 40 kilometers northwest of Riyadh.
Katif; Kateef	:	see Qatif
Kingdom of Saudi Arabia	:	the largest country of the Arabian Peninsula, occupying most of its central landmass.
Khuff, Al Khuffs	:	a hunting ground used by the Al Sauds located 200 kilometers west of Riyadh.
Kuwait, Kuweit	:	the name of both an emirate and its chief city located at the northwestern end of the Arabian Gulf.
Majma'ah, Mejma	:	a town located 200 kilometers northwest of Riyadh and 80 kilometers north of Shaqra.
Manama	:	main city on the northeast corner of Bahrain Island.
Marah, Meerad	:	a town 130 kilometers west-northwest of Riyadh and south of Shaqra.
Mecca, Macca, Makkah	:	the holiest city of Islam, the place of pilgrimage (*haj*), located midway north to south in the Hejaz, in the west of Saudi Arabia.

Medina	:	the second holiest city of Islam, the site of the tomb of the Prophet Mohammed (Peace be upon him), located 210 kilometers north of Mecca in the Hejaz.
Muwayh, Moiya	:	a town 200 kilometers north-northeast of Taif and 280 kilometers northeast of Jiddah.
Nefud Es Sirr, Nefud As Sirr	:	sandy desert region west of Riyadh, and immediately west of Nefud Qunayfidhah.
Najd, Nejd	:	the central deserts region of the Kingdom of Saudi Arabia.
Oneiza, Unayzah, Anieza	:	a town located 300 kilometers northwest of Riyadh.
Ojeir	:	see Uqair
Qatar, Katar	:	a peninsular country, an emirate jutting northward off the central east coastal region of the Arabian Peninsula.
Qatif, Qateef, Katif, Kateef	:	a port city on the east coast of Saudi Arabia north of Dammam.
Riyadh, Riadh	:	originally the capital city of Nejd, later of the Kingdom of Saudi Arabia; located very close to the center of the country.

Rukba Plains, Rukbah	:	an area of pasture lands in Hejaz between the towns of Al Muwayh and Ushayrah.
Shaqra, Shugra, Shukra	:	a town located 150 kilometers northwest of Riyadh.
Taif, Ta'if	:	a mountain town near Mecca in the Hedjaz, the western part of Saudi Arabia.
Tharmida, Thurmada	:	an oasis 140 kilometers west-northwest of Riyadh and south of Shaqra.
Trucial Coast	:	so called for a truce to refrain from sea warfare struck with Britain in 1853, this group of shaikhdoms on the southeast coast of Arabia later became the United Arab Emirates.
Uqair, Uqayr, Ojeir, Ojair	:	the customs port of Eastern Arabia in the days of Ottoman rule and later under the Al Sauds; a harbor almost directly west from the southern tip of Bahrain.
Uray'irah, 'Arier, Arrayrah	:	an oasis north of Hofuf on the old motor route to Riyadh.
Uwaynid, Awainid	:	an oasis 85 kilometers west-northwest of Riyadh.
'Uyaynah, Ainain	:	an oasis 45 kilometers northwest of Riyadh near Al Jubaylah.

Wadi Hanifa,

Wadi Hanifah,   :   a ravine running from the northwest of Riyadh, along its west side then south and southeast.

Wadi Jidda   :   an oasis on the motor route from Hofuf to Riyadh.*

Wadi Et Tairie,

Sha'ib At Tayri;   :   an oasis on the motor route from Hofuf to Riyadh.

Zallaq, Zallag   :   a port on the west coast of Bahrain.

Zilfi, Zulfie   :   a town 270 kilometers northwest of Riyadh at the north end of Jabal Tuwayk.

Bibliography

Archives of the Reformed Church in America:

    Russell L. Gasero, Archivist; Gardner Sage Library, New Brunswick
    Theological Seminary, New Brunswick, New Jersey, USA.

Arabian Mission:

    The Arabian Mission Field Reports, Nos. 1-26, 1892-1898
    The Arabian Mission Quarterly Letters from the Field, Nos. 27-40,
    1898-1901
    Neglected Arabia: Missionary News and Letters, Nos. 41-215,
    1901-1949
    Arabia Calling, Nos. 216-250, 1949-1962
    Reprinted by agreement with the Reformed Church in America as
    an eight volume set by Archive Editions, UK, 1988

Angela Clarke

The American Mission Hospital Bahrain: Through the Changing Scenes
of Life: 1893-1993; Manama, Bahrain;
The American Mission Hospital Society, Bahrain; 1993

Ann M. Harrison

A Tool in His Hand; New York, New York;
Friendship Press, Inc; 1958

Peter Mansfield
A History of the Middle East; New York, New York;
Penguin Group; 1991

Alfred DeWitt Mason & Frederick J. Barny
The History of the Arabian Mission; New York, New York;
The Board of Missions, R.C.A; 1926

Leslie McLoughlin
Ibn Saud: Founder of a Kingdom;
Houndmills, Basingstoke, Hampshire, UK;
The MacMillan Press Limited; 1993

C. Stanley G. Mylrea
Kuwait Before Oil -- the memoirs of Dr. C. Stanley G. Mylrea
(unpublished); 1951

Ismail I. Nawwab, Peter C. Spears, Paul F. Hoye-editors; Paul Lunde, John
A. Sabini, Lyn Maby-research & writing; *Aramco and its World: Arabia and
the Middle East;* Dhahran, Saudi Arabia; Aramco; 1981

Lewis R. Scudder III
The Arabian Mission's Story: In Search of Abraham's Other Son;
Grand Rapids, Michigan, USA; William B. Eerdmans Publishing Company;
1998

Samuel M. Zwemer & James Cantine
The Golden Milestone-Reminiscences of Pioneer Days Fifty Years Ago in Arabia;
New York, New York;
Fleming H. Revell Company; 1938

Maps

The Middle East; Skokie, Illinois, USA;
Rand McNally & Company; 1990

Middle East; Washington, District of Columbia, USA; National Geographic
Society; 1991

Saudi Arabia; Encarta Interactive World Atlas; Redmond, Washington, USA;
Microsoft Corporation; 2001

Atlas Maps : Kingdom of Saudi Arabia;
Zaki M.A. Farsi, Editor; Jedda, Saudi Arabia; 2002